DID GOD REALLY CALL YOU?

Why most ministers & church workers fail in the ministry.

E. S. Isaiah, Ph.D.

RECOMMENDATION

I would like to recommend this powerful book by Pastor Isaiah called "Did God really call you" to everyone. It does not matter whether you are a new believer or you are thinking of going into ministry as a young man or woman and even if you are already a pastor, this book is filled with so many insightful lessons to be learned.

I am recommending this book because I have known Pastor Isaiah for over 15 years now.

I remember back in 2007 when I met him in Houston, we were all young and in college but he was really different. His passion for God and the church stood out like a candle light in a dark room. He was so passionate about the things of God at a young age when most people were distracted by the world. He was the worship leader in the church and he would travel to different churches to lead worship. In my eyes then he was already a pastor, I am so happy that he never gave up on God despite all the challenges he faced. It blows my mind to see what God is doing through him today.

This book talks about the journey of a young man that has always been passionate about God and the church. I really liked how transparent and detailed he talked about his struggles. Most of all, I enjoyed reading about the stories of other ministers of the gospel who also struggled while ministering the gospel. I love the biblical references and stories as well, the took the chapters to another level spiritually.

Chapter 6 spoke personally to me. I read it twice because it talked about the struggle of doing God's work (your purpose on this earth) while trying to find the financial income to sustain you and your family. Also, the pressure to find the balance between getting a job and fulfilling your God given purpose on earth.

Finally, the three phrases I would use to describe this book are the following: God's Love, God's purpose for you his child and God's church.

Christie Echikwa, Ph.D

Dallas, Texas

Life Coach/Mentor/Motivational Speaker

Chapter eleven is apt and portrays that the divine impartation of the Holy Spirit is the discernable infusion of God in human beings, and accompanies the call to the pulpit or the leadings to work in God's Vineyard. Its indwelling grows with God's unction. Its operation in the life of the preacher/believer is that which becomes increasingly structured, noiseless, refined, clear, and ordered as the anointing grows. It guides us to emulate Jesus Christ, who was incorruptible, "went about doing good" (Acts 10: 38), yet was despised for it.

Chapter eleven is, therefore, an eloquent testimony and witness of the divinity of those who follow Christ to go about doing good, by the guidance of the Holy Ghost.

Professor Udo Moses Williams.

Former Nigerian Ambassador to Canada

DID GOD REALLY CALL YOU?

Paperback ISBN: 978-1-957809-37-3

Published by:
Cornerstone Publishing
A Division of Cornerstone Creativity Group LLC
Info@thecornerstonepublishers.com
www.thecornerstonepublishers.com

CONTACT INFORMATION

To order bulk copies of this book, please send an email to:
etyisaiah82@gmail.com

Printed in the United States of America.

FOREWORD

Servants of God are often assessed by the nature and strength of the individual gift or gifts given by the ascended Christ. It is understandable as these gifts are means by which the church grows to maturity.

Less frequently, servants of God are assessed on their character. God-given gifts will reach further and accomplish more when expressed through Christlike character which has been matured in times of testing.

Even less frequently, servants of God are assessed on their calling and Pastor Isaiah writes on this critically important matter in his book, 'Did God Really Call You?'.

In Romans 8, the Apostle Paul writes of a sequence of encounters in the lives of those chosen to be like His Son. They are chosen, called, made right and glorified. Each encounter is worthy of deep consideration and Pastor Isaiah deals with calling most seriously in his book which is a very personal account informed by the principles through which God calls his servants. These principles are illustrated by powerful, personal testimonies which provide a practical lens through which these eternal principles can be observed in one man's life.

The church has, since Pentecost, been critical to the wellbeing of humankind. Never more so than now and, at this juncture in human history, the church's ministry is vital. It's vitality is dependent upon its health and its health is dependent upon the quality of its leadership.

'Did God Really Call You?' is not about a lucrative career path, with security of tenure and the attendant benefits of secure employment. It is about a call so compelling that it can't be ignored. It is about a call so profound that demands a selfless response. Pastor Isaiah deals sensitively with a subject much misunderstood and challenges the called to a life of total surrender and complete abandonment to God's will – the only fitting response to the call of God.

I commend Pastor Isaiah as a passionate follower of Jesus Christ, an equipper of other who is, himself, equipped by gift, character and call. I commend his book 'Did God Really Call You?' as a significant contribution to the preparation of those called to serve the living God.

Pastor Timothy W. Jack

President Emeritus
The Apostolic Church, United Kingdom

DEDICATION

This book is dedicated to my Parents, Apostle S.A. Isaiah, Ph.D., and Deaconess A.S. Isaiah, who taught me all I know today about ministry and service to God. Also, to My Wife, Deaconess Myeshia Isaiah, for believing in the God who called me. I am forever grateful to you all.

CONTENTS

ACKNOWLEDGMENTS

My profound gratitude goes to my beautiful wife and our four angels for tolerating my absence at the dinner table and missing out on the PTA meetings and summer activities while gathering materials for the progress of this book. I love you Babe, Tye, Etimbuk Jr, Taelien and Iniubong. I will be forever grateful to my siblings and their Husbands (Elder & Deaconess Ibiok, Ms. Aniekeme, Arch. & Dr. (Mrs) Iyakeno Nnah, and Mr. David). Your love and support have made me who I am today. I love you all. To my Sister in the faith, Gwendolyn Yarbrough, thank you for pushing me to write this book after years of speculation and delay. Finally, to my Father in the Lord who took me in not minding my level in life, Apostle Okon A. Essien, Ph.D., and wife, God bless you.

I will never be able to repay you all for the love, teachings, and care throughout my years of service at your feet. It will be an injustice not to thank my best friends who, in one way or the other, helped in shaping the thoughts in this book. Janet Ofong, Manny Ekong, Uwana Whyte, Mfon Ofong, Inemesit Nwosu, Apostle MD Davies (UK), Pastor Emmanuel Umoh, My Parents In-Law (Deacon & Mrs. Gary Johnson), and my ever-loving Sister and Brother In-law (Mr. and Mrs. Lewis), for helping us with the children whenever they were called upon to. To my nieces and nephews, Dara, Edidiong, Enobong, Michelle, Grace, Zhylen, aka Bishop, and

Zhaire, thank you for trusting your Uncle with this book. One day, you will understand why I had to pen down my ministry experience.

Thanks to Dr. Pat Akpabio for time invested to review and edit the initial manuscript of this book.

I am eternally grateful to all my ministry partners worldwide (WWPP & PEIM) for all the prayers and support over the years. This book was inspired by the midnight prayers aired on Facebook and YouTube.

I saved the best for the last. My parents, Apostle Dr. & Deaconess S. A. Isaiah, deserve the most profound thanks for instilling in me the discipline I needed to become the Man after God's heart. Most of what is written in this book came from my many experiences with them. Thank you, Dad and Mom, for your unending support. I love you both.

INTRODUCTION

I sincerely appreciate you for taking out time to read this book. I am optimistic that this book will speak to you on a deep level and will exceed your expectations even before you finish reading it. Once more, many thanks!

"Did God Really call You?" is a book born out of the many experiences I have seen in the church as a young man serving in most church departments and even to the very top. So let's journey together and explore what God has for us as we travel through time with this book.

The numerous queries and unresolved issues that many new preachers today have encountered will be resolved in this book. I have studied what church leaders and preachers should and should not do. However, regardless of where and how you begin, this book will guide you to the appropriate sources and channels on how you should do things in the ministry to accomplish the correct objectives. Every young minister will encounter the challenges outlined in this book at some point in their lives, and I hope this book serves as a reminder that you are a victor no matter what.

I will stick with you through everything and examine the entire book together. Without those who foresaw and documented the myriad problems, an inexperienced person like you and me would not have had the opportunity to understand ministry as it is now.

As a youth Pastor and Sunday School Teacher for over ten years, I have closely observed and examined the factors that have suppressed the dreams and aspirations of our younger generation.

I have learned the many untold truths about God that our parents never shared with us, and as I grew older and gained more life experience, I knew what ministry was and was not. I was asked to take the lead in church ministries at a young age when the average age of the members was thirty to forty years older than I was. I remember my father's endless lessons and sermons when I was a young chorister, but I had nothing else to cling to or escape from.

My Pastor asked me to speak to a group of kids in 2017 about the life of Jesus when he was on earth. Thinking about the message kept me up at night while I contemplated how to start. It was a significant assignment that I knew would change my life, and I was willing to do my best. I immediately contacted my father to ask how he might assist me in beginning the task. He said over the phone, "Son, you ought to know this stuff by now." I could not think of anything to say in response to this statement since just hearing it gave me goosebumps. I respectfully asked him to give out the materials and sites I may utilize to start my teaching task. My father, a renowned scholar, highlighted so many Bible texts and other things throughout our conversation that my spirit man felt utterly energized.

I realized then that my journey as a young minister had just begun. I needed to spend more time studying the Scriptures as **Ecclesiastes 12:12 (KJV)** states, *"And further, my son, by these words be admonished: of making many books there is no end, and much study is a weariness of the flesh."*

A few other people and I were in tears on the day I finally taught the topic. After the powerful message, one of our members said, "Isaiah, it will be a sin and an injustice to the upcoming generation if you refuse to turn this teaching into a book."

Ladies and gentlemen, that is where the inspiration for this book first came to me in the spirit realm. It is crucial for any young person considering a career in ministry to realize that it is not a bed of roses. It is also important to remember that you will have to bear your burden and the crosses of others. So study the path of Jesus!

Let this book remain on your reading table, day and night. Act on it and pray with it as you read through the chapters day in and day out. It will solve your midnight cry and the many demands you will face in ministry, whether now or soon.

I hope you understand what I was thinking while writing this book and that it will meet your requirements and fulfill your desires. I am on your side, too! Let's journey together!

CHAPTER ONE
BORN TO A PREACHER

One of the many blessings in my life is knowing that God does not make mistakes in whatever he is doing. Many believe that once things go wrong in their lives, it indicates that God no longer cares about them. I will not say it was by chance, but God knew the assignment He had for me from the beginning, so he carefully picked where and when I would be born. He is a God of order. I firmly believe in *"Before I formed thee in the belly I knew thee, and before thou camest forth out of the womb I sanctified thee, and I ordained thee a Prophet unto the nations." (Jeremiah 5:1 KJV)* This Scripture gives me so much comfort and authority that nothing can take me away from the set-down will of God for my life.

Some people would not exchange their families for anything because of the love, support, and togetherness they experience. In contrast, others think they were born into the worst family on earth owing to the struggles they

1

face. However, a family with a solid foundation in God will always be successful. It is often said, "A family that prays together stays together."

This again points to God from the beginning to the end. Do you think God cares about family? Even in creation, He created Adam and Eve and then blessed them with children, showing his mindset about family and his plans for the family. Nobody goes to tell God what kind of family they would love to be born into or, better yet, tell God, "I want to change my family and be born into another family." We all grew up to see our parents, siblings, and other relatives. Some did not have both parents at all, but we were all born into a family either way.

Imagine a world where each of us had the freedom to select our parents. None of us, I believe, would choose a struggling family or one that has been shattered from top to bottom. The very best is what we will all pursue. God knew that I would become a Preacher one day and that I needed to be groomed; hence he placed me in the care of my parents. This is where that Scripture comes to the whole reality "...I knew thee and ...I ordained thee." Get this word in your spirit as you read this book. **YOU ARE NOT A MISTAKE!** Regardless of the circumstances and challenges, never assume that God must have made a mistake by allowing you to be born into that family.

Declare this: I am a blessed child, and my destiny is assured.

THE BIRTH

In my little experience as a Pastor, I have been blessed to listen to and hear many birth stories: some painful, some teary, and some with a smile. However, I have inferred from all those endless birth stories that the mothers are always delighted to have their babies, disregarding the agonizing pains and labor they had to endure. There is something so profound about the birth of a child. This is the blessing of every mother, no matter the age and stage. Therefore, in my quest to know more about my birth, I sat my father down with the help of some of my staff to ask some questions surrounding my birth.

Knowing that I was about to hear the tale of how I was born, I could see his face light up with anticipation. My parents had several prophetic messages about my birth, and from my conversation with Dad, I learned that he had wanted male children first and then female afterward. But God knew the plans ahead of them and gave them a female child first, then a male child followed.

I was born on a Sunday morning while folks were preparing for church. Maybe that is one of the reasons Sunday is my favorite day of the week. When the news of my birth reached my Dad, who was at home preparing for the Sunday service, he was overly excited and gave me the name "Etimbuk," which means "Good News." As I mentioned earlier, my grooming and mentoring started from birth from a father and mother who were constantly praying and fasting for the glory of God to be manifested in me as a child of promise.

In my understanding of the Scripture, there are three things in the life of every child born into the world: a destiny, a star, and a blessing. These things must walk hand in hand in a child's life, and whenever any of these aforementioned is missed, then the life and future of such a child begin to darken. But, on the other hand, nothing brings me joy more than seeing a child who has lived up to God's full potential in their life. My parents would often leave us in a room to fast and pray for the purpose and glory of God to be revealed to us as children.

I honestly believe that was the beginning of my journey to ministry. I had to go through the preparation level, knowing fully well that God saw what would happen thirty-plus years ahead of me, even before I could smell or see it. Look at God! I can state that most Preacher's Kids (PK) in our churches never received the same exposure to their fathers as I did.

I attended many conventions, church rallies, and prayer sessions and met many leaders standing next to my father or sitting on the hardwood pews in church back in Africa. Even though, as a little boy, I did not fully understand what was happening. I so much enjoyed the services, and I would never want them to end. But as a child, I barely hung on to the end of every service as my infant eyes would fight nature, and the spirit of sleep would tempt me until I gave in. Then, waking up in the comfort of my bed, I would ask how I got there from sitting in the pews at church. All I could get as an answer was that the service was over, and I was carried to the car. But childhood came with some fun stuff.

As I grew, I longed for the things of God. I knew God had given me a gift, and thankfully, He gave me parents who helped nurture that gift. What has God placed in your life as a gift? Please find it and develop it to become a reality for you. God does not give gifts for us to sit on. He gives us things that will help others and also, in return, bless us with the instrument. If a farmer plants and all he does is harvest and sell his crops without eating them, how will he know he has done a great job on his farm? God wants you to use the gift inside of you to its full potential. Stop waiting for others to tell you what to do with what God gave you.

He trusted you enough to carry on with the gift, hence the reason behind him giving you the advantage. It is in you, PUSH! Sometimes, birth is the most challenging part of the process. After birth, all other things will begin to fall into place.

There is a king or queen in you. You have waited too long, and it is your time now to push. By the end of this journey, you will gain enough momentum that will spark your spirit man into doing the impossible and the unthinkable. I know you will excel and will do great.

III John 1:2 "Beloved, I wish above all things that thou mayest prosper and be in health, even as thy soul prospereth." (KJV)

A journey without God is a wasted journey and a wasted life. In the next chapter, I will point out what God will do when you commit your journey to Him and when He becomes the pilot of your plane.

5

CHAPTER TWO
CHURCH OR NOTHING

I believe that I can use the words of David as declared in *Psalms 122:1 "I was glad when they said unto me, let us go into the house of the Lord."* These words here are more of a reporting statement, but it was an experience of a lifetime for me. Living with my parents meant that I had to attend church regardless of how I felt. While some of those services were painful to sit through, some I would wish never came to an end. Attending countless morning devotional services, choir rehearsals, men's meetings, Sunday school classes, musicians rehearsals, and much more was a routine for my siblings and me.

It was wrong to stay in the church mission house while church service was ongoing, and it usually attracted beatings from Dad. He also encouraged us to have a total commitment to various church departments. In today's world, some children would consider that abuse, while others would find ways to move out of the house so they can be free to do whatever they want and however they want. Regardless of where you were at any given time as a young teenage boy, Dad's rule was the church or nothing. It would be justifiable to say that my siblings and I were genuine church caretakers, not because we lived inside the church mission house but because we loved doing the things of God.

ONE DAY, YOU WILL BECOME

As a preacher's kid (PK), you would hear many people say, "you will be like your father." Those words were somewhat frightening as my heart would leap in fear looking at the crowd of people and the size of the church. There were scholars, lawyers, teachers, government workers, academia, doctors, nurses, Ph.D. holders, and the best of the best in the church who, by a slip of the tongue, would quickly know that you have not been studying to show yourself approved as the Bible states in II Timothy 2:15.

Yes, I always wanted to be like Dad, even mimicking his dance steps as a little boy. But the only part I did not want to do was preach in front of the people with all eyes fixed on me, watching my every step and lifestyle.

As the service progressed, I would squirm around on the mat next to my mother while asking myself many questions. I was aware of the call of God upon my life, but the terror I felt was primarily related to PEOPLE rather than my own experiences or the numerous unresolved questions that persisted in my mind.

This is what happened to Moses when he faced the Red Sea. He had the miracle and the answer in his hands, but instead, he allowed the people and the crowd to push him into wondering if the God (Who sent him to Egypt) would come through for him and the children of Isreal.

Young Man and Woman, do not be afraid; one day, you will BECOME! The Scripture states it very clearly,

For the vision is yet for an appointed time, but at the end, it shall speak, and not lie: though it tarries, wait for it; because it will surely come, It will not tarry. (Habakkuk 2:3 KJV)

Everything in life happens at the appointed time, and no matter how much you push and jump all curves, what will be will be! There is no easy way to succeed. Learn to work hard and bring God on board in all your affairs. As recorded in the Scripture, "Draw nigh to God, and he will draw nigh to you. Cleanse your hands, ye sinners; and purify your hearts, ye double minded." (James 4:8 KJV)

Let this be your moment to think deeply and revisit that part of your life that has lost connection with the church. It will surprise you that most of today's secular artists were once choir members and church praise team leaders. Along the line, something happened to them in church, leaving a bitter taste in their mouth and the wrong concept about God. Go back to that church and ministry God has placed in your hands. Do not reflect on the past or let material possessions consume you. Seek God first, and He shall add other things to you. I am who I am today, not because my parents were believers but because I knew God for myself, and I kept to that word in my life. David, who knew the God he served, said, "I was glad..."

He was excited to be in the house of God. That speaks volumes about his personality as a Man after God's heart.

I wish, above all, that you will hear and understand the mind of God concerning you and what is ahead for your life. I speak to that spirit inside of you to gain strength and passion for the things of God again and walk into your calling, knowing fully well that one day, YOU WILL BECOME!

Generations yet unborn are lined up to hear your voice. Do not disappoint God!

CHAPTER THREE

GETTING TO KNOW GOD

here is a saying, "One tree can never form a forest."
I believed this idiomatic expression was only for
the trees and nothing else. But, of course, I was
dead wrong in my understanding. One of my instructors
in our Biblical College years ago once told me, *"Isaiah, no
matter how good and prolific of a person or writer you are, if you
do not have a successor or somebody to hand over your robes to, then
you are a failure in life."*

But wait! I thought we were all running this race by
ourselves? So why do I need somebody to carry on from
where I stopped? This is a question of WHEN? WHO?
And HOW? In this chapter, I will dig deeper into these
three key questions.

Many people in today's society do not believe in
grooming the next generation. Some do not think that
the same God using them can also use a small boy in the
streets. Gone are the days when people say you are too
young to lead, preach or teach in a church. God can use
anyone. David was thirty years old when he became King.

At thirty, God would have said, "you are too young to lead my people," but no, it was in the will of God even before his birth. Our forefathers failed to understand that God does not call the QUALIFIED, but he QUALIFIES the called.

God is not waiting for you to become a full-grown married man or woman for Him to use you or find you worthy for a minister's office. The voices of mentors and fathers in the lord have killed many youths in the church who told them they were too young to lead. From that moment, the quest for honest self-evaluation began.

I believe I was seven years old when my parents showed and taught us about God, what makes God happy, and what God hates. I can still recall my father showing us colors from a piece of cloth (White-purity, Red-the-blood of Jesus, Black-Our Sins before him, White-Our clean heart). He took time to explain each color's significance and its role in our walk with God.

From that point on, I understood what God despised and what he loved. After those teachings, my father will take time to pray and lay hands on us. As young as I was, I heard his lines and words, asking God to use us even from a young age.

Nobody is too young to know God. Samuel was called at a young age, and what baffles me with the story of Samuel is that Eli did not recognize that it was God calling Samuel. At his age, as a seasoned Man of God, it took him three trials to finally awaken to the fact that it could be God trying to get Samuel's attention. Finally, Samuel heard the voice of God, but Eli's ears were too heavy to hear.

God will show you things he will not deliver to your Pastor, Bishop, Evangelist, Prophet, etc. That does not mean he does not want to communicate with them, but he is interested in you at that moment and time.

Revelation 20:12 "And I saw the dead, small and great, stand before God; and the books were opened: and another book was opened, which is the book of life: and the dead were judged out of those things which were written in the books, according to their works." (KJV)

This indicates that God will judge everyone according to their works here on earth. This is the time to know God for yourself while you still have strength. My father once told me, "That I am a Pastor does not save you or give you an automatic ticket to heaven. You must know God for yourself." His job was to point me on the right path and tell me everything I had to know about God and his love for me. My part was to accept and believe that he is a rewarder of those who diligently seek him. This process does not stop here; I also teach my children this strategy. Remember now thy Creator in the days of thy youth, while the evil days come not, nor the years draw nigh when thou shalt say, I have no pleasure in them. (Ecclesiastes 12:1)

Now is the right time to know God; do not forget

that tomorrow is never promised to anyone. So the question is, do you know God? What is your relationship like with him now?

DOUBLE STANDARD

Unfortunately, a lot of individuals in the current generation no longer have the fear of God in them. People do and say things that make you question the existence of God, even in the church. I hear and read so many stories and breaking news about preachers killing people; some go as far as committing suicide. The question that races through my mind is, do they know God? What could drive a preacher to commit suicide? The answer is simple: They had no "personal" relationship with God. I pray you do not become a victim. If you notice, my keyword there is PERSONAL.

Yes, they heard about God and how loving and caring He is, but they had no one-on-one encounter with God like Samuel, Moses, Abraham, David, and the rest of the people in the Bible did. So because of this, they struggled in ministry without a proper guide. Some rushed into the church because they saw it as a way of surviving and meeting ends.

According to the Pastoral mental health report magazine, published on July 15th, 2021, "More than 1 in 10 pastors admitted to contemplating suicide in the past year."

40% of pastors between the ages of 25 and 40 reported feeling burned out, with about 35% of pastors frequently feeling this way. This is nearly double the rate at which pastors aged 60-plus reported feeling burned out (21%). (https://rushtopress.org/9111-2/)

If this is not alarming to you, then I do not know what else would. Part of the problem is they were not nurtured or taught the ways and deeds of God. Nobody mentored them, and some under mentorship never cared to listen or take heed.

THE KEY

You are never too young or old to know God. God does not have an age requirement. That is why the Preacher (Ecclesiastes) states clearly, "Remember NOW," not tomorrow or another day, but NOW. There is room for you to know this God I speak about. Your father's relationship with God will NOT save you or guarantee you a spot in Heaven should your life end today.

You must have a personal relationship with him and him alone. He is calling you, yes YOU. Give your life to him today. You are never too young to know God.

My prayer for you today is that you will accept Jesus as your Lord and Savior and allow him to come into your heart and be the Lord of your heart. He will direct your affairs and guide every move you make. Once this occurs, you will attest to God's intervention in your life. I have never regretted knowing God. He has been a father since I accepted him as my Lord and Savior. So join me today, and let us make this decision together again.

Repeat after me:

Lord Jesus, come into my heart; I repent of all my sins and acknowledge you as my Lord and Savior. Take charge. I surrender all to you from this day onward. I want to live for you and you alone, cleanse me, and make me a new person. I pray in Jesus' name, Amen.

Congratulations, you are now a new creature in Christ!

CHAPTER FOUR
THE JOURNEY BEGINS

I want you to know this and get it in your spirit; every word that God spoke concerning you will all come to pass, no matter the obstacle or what is delaying it. For example, I stated that I had to come to know God for myself earlier in the previous chapter. Yes, it was okay that I had a father and mother who taught me all I needed to know about God, but I wanted to explore that part of myself that others did not know. At a very young age, I was asked to preach in Sunday school rallies at church, and I can vividly remember how my teachers would bring a small podium and place it right where the lantern was so I could be seen once I stepped on the pulpit.

I would stand there with my Sunday school teacher behind me as a bodyguard, cheering me on to say what I had practiced for almost a month or two. As much as I was scared to make mistakes, I knew my father was seated behind me, and my Sunday school teacher was just a whisper away from my ears.

That was the confidence I needed. Before you get

excited on my behalf, let me break the sad news to you. When my teachers knew I had mastered the art and could absorb the eyes of more than five hundred worshippers looking at me, they allowed me to stand on my own. They gradually stopped coming on stage, knowing that I was no more terrified of the audience or anybody observing from behind.

I honestly believe this is where my grooming in ministry began. I was eventually selected to speak the word at rallies, not because I was the pastor's child but because of what my Sunday school teachers saw in me. It is good to be involved in the things of God. I am a living witness that God will remember your works and services before him. No matter what, God does not forget.

God's promises in your life will surely come to pass. When I left the shores of Nigeria back in 2003, I had no relatives in the United States whatsoever, but I had God. I arrived in Oklahoma, where I attended college, and saw God's hands manifesting again. I joined the Methodist Church there, and every Sunday, we would gather at the Pastor's house to wait for the church van to transport us to the church, which was thirty minutes away from campus.

In one of our Sunday services, the Late Pastor Jay Lark of blessed memory grabbed my hands and said, "You guys from Africa can preach, and I know you got a word. So, I am putting you to preach next Sunday on the roster." Before I could compose myself to absorb what he had just said to me, the seventy-four-year-old man walked away. His statement shook everything in me. So many thoughts came to me. What will I say?

How will I be able to talk in front of these white men and women who may not comprehend a single word I say because of my thick Nigerian accent? At some point, I had wanted to call in and make an excuse, but Pastor Lark was also a lecturer in the school I attended, and he knew pretty much everyone there as an agriculturist. My world came to a standstill, and I ran out of time.

To worsen the situation, he broadcasted the news of my preaching to every student on campus as if the mayor was coming to service that day. I lost my appetite for food, had sleepless nights, and went digging into my Sunday school notes from back home (Nigeria) to see if I could find anything worth sharing with the church on Sunday. At last, the big day arrived, and the church was packed to the brim. I was on the pulpit with other campus pastors who had come to hear a black African boy preach, which had never happened before in the church's history.

Before the pastor called me to deliver the message God had laid upon in my heart, Pastor Lark, who sat next to me, held my hand and said, "You got this, and I am here with you." Believe me, when he said this, those were the most calming words I had ever heard in my life besides the voice of God. When I stepped onto the podium, I spoke from the book of Esther, chapter 6, one of my favorite Scriptures. I took time and went through everything thoroughly. During my preaching, I saw an older woman sobbing, and men fought back emotions as they kept their eyes on me throughout the service.

I could hear Late Pastor Lark clapping and cheering me on, *"Come on, Isaiah preach. Say it, Son."* What I felt was like pouring fuel into a fire that was already raging.

I forgot where I was and went in as the spirit led me that cold winter Sunday. After the sermon, the Late Pastor Lark came to me in the minister's room, where I was ushered in immediately after my sermon as the custom of the church for every preacher, and he said to me, *"You have been chosen to lead the youth department of this church henceforth."* I was so stunned and dumbfounded that I could not help but cry when I asked him how he accomplished it without consulting the church board of directors or a formal interview, which was the church doctrine.

He chuckled and said, "Haven't we seen how God has used you today?" He shook my hands and said, "Congratulations to you, Minister Isaiah." That was the first place I was officially given the title **"Minister."** At this point, I formally began my quest to realize my true potential. I assumed leadership of the church's youth department. Knowing how to sing and play the piano was an added advantage. The young people there took me in, not minding if I was black or from Africa. I could see myself as a Pastor because I was saddled with the responsibility of drawing out a lesson plan for the youths and young adults, and the church trusted me enough to lead in that office.

That sermon was talked about throughout my entire school year in Oklahoma until the day I left. I had this experience in all the churches I joined (only two in Oklahoma). Foursquare Bible Church in Guymon, Oklahoma, did the same thing to me, took me under their wings and nurtured me as the only black man in the church. I was loved and cared for. The church would visit my dorm room several times and bring me snacks and food. It was a season of learning and coaching for me simultaneously.

I witnessed God's hand guiding and protecting me as I grew from childhood to adulthood. That office of a Minister came with so many responsibilities, making decisions and sound judgment on things, and not to mention that I was allowed to join the church board of directors meeting where they asked questions about my departments and the wellbeing of my youths. This helped shape who I am today as I journeyed through life as a Man, A preacher's kid, and a student in school.

DO NOT BE

God's word is truthful and comforting on every side. God says in *John 14:18, "I will not leave you comfortless: I will come to you." (KJV)*

God is communicating to you personally in your times of fear and need. You have no reason to be afraid or scared of the unknown. He states it very clearly, "I WILL NOT." He will never take the initiative to accomplish this. So what is holding you from taking that step in ministry or your life? Until you take that bold step, nothing will change or happen.

Jesus said to Peter, *"Come on the water" (Matthew 14:28-29).*

One of the rare places in the Bible where I perceive Jesus as having a great sense of humor is at this particular point. He did not tell Peter "No." Instead, he said, "Come," since you want to test the powers within you,

21

no problem, I am here with you all the way. It is rather sad that even when Peter knew the Man who spoke to him and the power he possessed, Peter gave up on faith too soon just looking at the water, and you know what happened to him next. He began to sink.

Many times in our lives as young Ministers, God is giving us a pathway to walk and do his will, but we are too caught up with the winds of our lives and the troubles ahead of us. But, if we can trust Jesus, then and only then will everything be okay. So, take that step of faith, knowing he has your back any day.

This journey will not be an easy one. Please hear me as you read this book. Yes, there are untold stories of what I went through as a young minister, and I will do my best to tell them in this book, but never assume that everything will be smooth because you are working for God. The reverse is the case. Get mentors and leaders that will guide you on the right path. I cannot tell you how many times I have had to call my Dad to ask him about something in the Bible that I needed clarity on, and thank God he was always there to guide me through it.

Although this may not apply to you specifically, believe me when I say that God has someone who will serve as your mentor and life coach. Take that bold step today, and you will be amazed at what God can and will do for you. It is often said that "the journey of a thousand miles begins with a step." Take that step today!

CHAPTER FIVE

GOD SET A TRAP

Twenty-five years ago, if anyone had told me that I would one day become a preacher of the word, I would have gotten in a fight with such a person. I saw firsthand what my father went through in ministry as a pastor. The insults, the endless meetings, the many travels, the night prayers, and no time for rest, but he endured them all. That was not the kind of life I wanted and dreamt of. I knew from the beginning of time that I had always wanted a profession that I could speak at will, and that was International Relations. Never in my wildest dream did I ever fathom in my mind that God had something different from what my plans were.

"For I know the thoughts I think toward you, saith the LORD, thoughts of peace, and not of evil, to give you an expected end." (Jeremiah 29:11 KJV)

What we fail to understand in life is that God gets to make the final decision no matter what we want in life. He wants to give you an expected end to fit what he planned for you from the onset. Many preachers today are doctors, lawyers, university teachers, etc., and can still function as pastors or church leaders in their offices. I honestly thought ministry was over when I left Nigeria, but little did I know that it was just getting started upon my arrival in America. God only brought me to another land to do the same thing I would have done in Nigeria. After preaching in my church in Oklahoma, I found myself constantly searching the Bible in preparation for the next church meeting day. My taste for the word increased, and I would not go a day without spending at least an hour studying the word of God. My roommate Hillary Nkemchap, from Cameroon, gave me the nickname "Pope."

Even after my school years in Oklahoma, the majority of the newcomers in school never knew my real name. From speaking in one service to leading a church youth department, God was carefully taking me to that place he had for me, but I was busy trying to get a degree in International Relations. God knew I wanted to be a prolific speaker, so he aligned me with his purpose, which was to preach the word of God. Is that not a talking job? Yes, it is.

God has an enormous sense of humor. Left for me, I would have wrestled my way through that decision, but God knew a day like this would come when you have to read through the lines of this book and see for yourself that He is a promise keeper. That was the trap he set for me, knowing I would fall into it and be caught up with it. Given my past life, I do not know what could have become of me. Thank you, Lord, for the trap you set in my path.

Maybe you find yourself shuffling between a secular job and ministry work and debating which one to let go of or hang on to. Pay attention to what God is saying; I beg you to listen and act on it when he speaks. The clouds may be hovering over you now, and you feel like throwing in the towel, but let me assure you that God will never give up on you, no matter the circumstance.

I can boldly say today that God has never left me since I started this journey with him. There are dark days and moments when the spirit is willing, but the flesh is weak. As Paul, the Apostle, states in II Corinthians 12: 9,

"And He said to me, "My grace is sufficient for you, for My strength is made perfect in weakness. Therefore, most gladly, I will rather boast in my infirmities that the power of Christ may rest upon me." (KJV)

What you currently do as a job or trade may not be what you will end up doing for the rest of your life on earth. Remember, the disciples of Jesus were fishermen, tax collectors, physicians, etc., but at the end of the day, Jesus called them all to become fishers of Men. Are you ready to fight off the fear of the unknown? What is the one thing that is holding you from making that decision? If you are indeed called to serve, you will always find yourself at the place of service, no matter what. Let me point out something: haven't you noticed that every time you do something in your church or ministry, people admire you and wish you had the whole year to do it over and over again?

People don't get bored hearing you preach, sing, or teach. What do you think is going on? You're not Whitney Houston or TD Jakes. This is not your fault. Only God's grace and your calling are at work. Period!

I know the road will not be easy, but I promise God will always be there. Adversaries will come, and people will push buttons, but God will give you the grace to overcome.

According to Barna, an online news outlet, in 2021, 38% of U.S. Pastors thought of quitting their entire time in ministry. This number calls for prayer, given that we are speaking about Pastors, Men, and Women of faith who should encourage others to hold onto God and not give up. But, unfortunately, the enemy is after your mind and wants you to play a role in his plan.

CHAPTER SIX

I THINK I AM LOSING IT!

O ne of the things I had to learn all by myself was that sometimes God would not give you all you need and want. It took me some time to understand Matthew 6:11 in its entirety. *"Give us this day our daily bread," KJV.* Notice that it did not say, "Give us every day our daily bread." It only requested a daily bread per day and what will last for that day only. Sometimes in life, we ask God for something that will not benefit us for today or the next two months. There is a lot of competition in the body of Christ that has ruined many things and torn apart the true essence of worship. I used to ask God for many things at once, and God, on the other hand, was trying to tell me to be precise. SPECIFICITY is the key to accessing what you need in the kingdom of God. You can't float your request and expect God to answer all because it is you who is asking.

I would preach many nights and days in revivals, and deep inside me, I was struggling with a need that I wanted God to help me with. But unfortunately, I had no secular job and applied to all the jobs I thought I qualified for, but all I got in return was declines and rejections. Despite this, I still had to wake up, get dressed in my suit, and head to the revival or travel to the next preaching gig to tell others that God will never fail in his words or promises. Deep inside, I was losing my mind because I had no job.

I can speak from a personal experience on this. After I finish preaching, healing and deliverance will take place in our services, men and women will come to know the Lord, and I will leave at the end of it all back to my hotel room to hear the enemy say, "You still do not have a job, Sir." These seasons in my life as a preacher were the turning point for me, and I had to wrestle with voices and depression with the hope that God would soon come to my aid. There were nights when I would preach, receive no compensation, and sometimes depart with less than $200. I remember ministering in worship for one week for a pastor who came in from Nigeria, and these services lasted till 2 am the next day.

At the end of it, all I could get from the preacher was, "God bless you, Sir." Yes, I believe in God's blessings, but the question was, "WHY?" Why can't He pass through people like them to bless me financially? I would leave those meetings angry and upset at God and the preacher for not giving me anything in return.

I was honestly losing it and needed to know what I was doing wrong that made God shut the heavens on me as his servant. One day while I was praying in the morning, I heard God say to me, "Be specific." I paused as it was as if I heard some footsteps in the house, and

God repeated it, "Be Specific," then this Scripture quickly came to me, *"So Jesus stood still, called them, and said, "What do you want Me to do for you?"* (Matthew 20:32 KJV)

God took the veil off my eyes at the place of prayer, and I instantly asked God for a specific job I wanted. Two weeks later, I received a phone call from one of my old colleagues asking me if I was interested in working for a particular company that had just opened in the area. I immediately said yes and sent in my resume. To my surprise, they hired me instantly after an interview over the phone. I had seen firsthand the result of being specific in the place of prayer, and it worked. Most Christians pray for years and do not get the result of what they prayed for because of a lack of specificity in their devotion. You cannot believe God for one million dollars, and then you tell God, "give me some money." You have to be specific with the amount you want. Remember, He is a God of order.

From that moment when I realized that my prayer needed to be targeted at something and could not just be broad, I started seeing results.

In the story of the two blind men who sat by the roadside, everyone knew they were blind, even Jesus himself. So Jesus asked that question, "what do you want me to do for you?" They could have wanted money or food, but they asked that their sight be restored.

I was preaching at a revival in a Baptist Church in Nyack, New York, in March 2016. While I was preaching, there was a lady in her late twenties seated right in front of me, and I noticed that she was crying all through the service while I was preaching. After the sermon, the holy spirit told me to go into worship, and I quickly did. As I was in the mood for prayer, the Lord said to me that the lady needed a child and that her marriage was on the verge of crashing due to this. So, the Lord instructed me to ask her how many children she wanted to have in her marriage.

I stopped the song I was singing, called her out, and asked her the question. With uncontrollable tears rolling down her face, she said, "I want twins, a boy and a girl." I told her to reach out in faith and take them. But, instead, she did what I have never in my thirty-plus years in ministry seen any woman do. She stretched forth her hands as if she were collecting something from me and placed one on her right shoulder and another on her left shoulder. Suddenly her face lit up. She cleaned her tears and returned to her seat. That was the end, and I forgot about my encounter with her. Fast forward to 2018. I was invited again by the same pastor to preach.

After service, as the church's security was escorting me to my car, I heard somebody screaming, "Pastor Isaiah, Pastor Isaiah, please stop, please stop." I halted, and I could recall the face as I turned around. She immediately handed me a baby wrapped in a pink blanket while a young lady held another baby in a blue blanket. She paused and looked at me with tears as she pointed to the baby in my hands. "This is the miracle God used you to do in my family." I asked her, "Who are you again?" She smiled and replied, "The lady you prayed for to have twins." I knew right there and then that God had answered her prayers.

She was specific with her request. Nobody walks into a restaurant and begins to scream, "Give me food." You have to look at the menu and see what they have or ask the waiter what type of food is available for the day and then make your choice. This is how we should approach God in place of prayer. Do not be broad, be specific!

I was losing my mind because I had no idea how to approach God in my place of prayer. People would come to me and tender their prayer requests (Specific prayers), and I would use that to pray with them, and God would answer right away. Still, in my case, I thought He was not interested and had turned a deaf ear to my prayers. The story of Naomi, Ruth, and Orpah serves as a reminder that God rewards those who wait on him. Take a look at this, "But Ruth said: "Entreat me not to leave you, or to turn back from following after you; For wherever you go, I will go; And wherever you lodge, I will lodge; Your people shall be my people, And your God, my God." (Ruth 1:16 KJV)

Naomi knew very well there was no way she would be able to give birth to children anymore for her daughters-in-law to marry, so she advised them to go home and start life all over. Ruth refused, but Orpah kissed her mother-in-law goodbye and walked away. Ruth knew that if she held on a bit longer, she would get something out of it. Thank God for women like Ruth. From her lineage comes Jesus, who will save the world from their sins. Learn to be specific no matter what. Tell the lord precisely what it is you need and trust him to do it.

THE POWER OF SPECIFICITY

You have to realize that prayer is a weapon you must use correctly. Unfortunately, many ministers abuse prayer, some turn it into a moment of speaking in tongues, and some play over it. You will become a failure IF you do not understand the power of SPECIFICITY in the place of prayer.

I have taught my church and youths that you cannot approach God with a broad mind. God wants us to be specific. Ask yourself how other tribes and races get breakthroughs with little to nothing, sometimes no fasting or tedious prayer sessions. Not binding and losing, yet they get a breakthrough when they pray? The answer is they know how to be specific with their prayer.

"Ministry is not a bed of roses," Dad always says. You will have moments where you pray for the needs of others while you suffer and bleed in silence. My word of encouragement to you is, do not lose your mind. In the fullness of time, God will do it. Remember, God is not a man, and all he says is true. I pray that in your dark days as a minister of the gospel and as you struggle to hear God speak in your time of pain, He will grant you the grace to hold on and not give up.

CHAPTER SEVEN

WHO CALLED YOU?

When I read the story of Samuel and Eli, I tend to do two things, laugh and cry. Even the Bible says, "...The word of God was rare." Meaning it was not accessible to some. Eli was God's big-time servant and a seasoned Man of God. Samuel lived with him as an aid. What baffles me most in the story of Samuel and Eli is that Eli did not sense God was trying to get Samuel's attention. Perhaps you would say that his ears were heavy or old age. "Then the Lord called yet again, "Samuel!" So Samuel arose, went to Eli, and said, "Here I am, for you called me." He answered, "I did not call, my son; lie down again." (I Samuel 3:6 KJV)

Eli was almost blind and in the temple, with Samuel serving him in his last days. It took Eli three attempts before he could sense that God was trying to get Samuel's attention. The fascinating part of this story is that Samuel did not yet have the word, nor was God's

33

word revealed to him. "Now Samuel did not yet know the Lord, nor was the word of the Lord yet revealed to him." (I Samuel 3:7 KJV)

He was in the temple (Church as you would call it today), but he (Samuel) had not yet known God or had the word of God in his mouth. I have often come across ministers who speak the word of God based on their educational background and NOT the biblical content written down in the Scriptures. Some add what they know works for them, and some mix it to fit their narrative. When I see things of this nature, I question a lot of things and the authenticity of that minister.

Some called themselves into ministry, and some came in because that was the only way to survive and make a living. Others went into the ministry for selfish reasons or material things with no anointing or message for the people of God. Because they came from behind, they struggle to be relevant and known, and when that does not work, they soil their hands in fetish things and charms to make a name.

I know of many pastors that have never opened a Bible to preach or teach but will do miracles as if it were their last day on earth. Vanity upon vanity! The call of God is without repentance. God does not call anyone and then regret ever using that person.

But on the other hand, some people have become a disgrace at work and have left many questioning who called them.

In today's church, you will see a lot of strange doctrines and practices that do not align with the word of God, and people pour into it in thousands. Quick deliverance, money schemes, and arranged and staged miracles are all in the name of God, and the sad part is that they open the Bible to preach about God to the same people they just lied to. It makes you ask, "who called them?" I know you would say we are not supposed to judge, but the Scripture says it clearly at the end of the day. "...And the truth shall set you free."

One of the prayers I always prayed was, "God, if you genuinely called me, then show me your glory and presence wherever I go and whenever I stand to speak your word." Why do we think God is no more powerful than he was when he intervened on behalf of the three Hebrew boys and protected Daniel by shutting the mouths of lions?

I attended a Manpower Conference hosted by Bishop TD Jakes, and he gave this powerful quote that changed my life forever. *"TO BE PUBLICLY POWERFUL, YOU MUST BE PRIVATELY PRAYERFUL."*

Whatever is not from God will NEVER last. Let me say that again, whatever is not from God will never stand. Regardless of how prominent you are today or how effectively you disguise yourself publicly, God will reveal you when the time comes. Seek his presence and glory, and you will see him in full splendor. "And I will give you shepherds according to My heart, who will feed you with knowledge and understanding." (Jeremiah 3:15 KJV)

A day after my ordination as a full-time pastor, my Father called me into his hotel room. I knew right then that he wanted to speak to me about ME. I sat on the sofa in his room, watching him drink his early morning tea. Then, as usual, he suddenly cleared his throat and began to speak. One of the things he said that stood out so deeply to me was this. "Son, only three things will bring you down in ministry from what I have come to see and know in my years of being a Pastor. Money, Women, and Charms."

Dad began to speak these words as if he was reading them from a newspaper, and I sat at the edge of the sofa, listening with rapt attention. He was pretty specific in telling me that if any of the things above occurred and I failed or fell short in ministry, the same people who had formerly praised and hailed me would doubt my anointing and wonder if God had called me. As much as I would love to go into details about what Dad said, I will say this; it was the most defining moment for me in ministry to hear those words from my biological father, and I did not take it for granted.

Pastors, bishops, and other men and women of God come to the church unprepared. Some sit on the altar looking and flipping through the Bible for what to preach to the church in that same service. Some rely on google for a sermon somebody else has already preached, and because it was not given to them by God, they fumble and cannot deliver it as they would have if the spirit led them. Many have become noise makers on the pulpit, making blunders here and there. They confuse themselves and others with their philosophy. Because they did not

36

wait for God to provide the appropriate message to the people, they will preach one thing today and then return the next day to retract their remarks.

God will never leave you alone. When he sends you, he always follows through on his promises. Your call must come with signs and wonders (Not fake ones). The people must attest that God is using you as a vessel to work in his vineyard. Please take a look at what happened to Paul the Apostle while he was preaching.

> *"And in a window sat a certain young man named Eutychus, sinking into a deep sleep. He was overcome by sleep, and as Paul continued speaking, he fell from the third story and was taken up dead. And Paul went down, fell on him, and embracing him, said, "Do not trouble yourselves, for his life is in him." Now when he had come up, had broken bread and eaten, and talked a long while, even till daybreak, he departed." (Acts 20:9-11 KJV)*

Eutychus fell asleep as some of us do in our churches. Paul was preaching, not noticing that one of his members had dozed off into another realm. Perhaps Eutychus just returned from work and decided to attend service, or maybe he was just one who would stay awake to dance and scream in church but sleep during the sermon. I am also tempted to believe that the house must have been filled to the brim, and the only space available was by the window, and Brother Eutychus decided to squeeze his little self into that space to get some fresh air.

The Bible does not tell us what made him fall asleep. But here is the deal, he fell asleep and fell to his death on the third floor of the building, something so tragic. How do you go to the presence of God and return home dead? Eutychus had become so comfortable where he was sitting that he thought it wise to fall asleep, not minding the outcome.

That fresh air felt so good that he let go of himself and suddenly landed dead at the bottom of the building. Wait for a second! Do you mean he died? Yes, he did. Paul served as a vehicle for God to demonstrate that He called him at this point. The Bible says Paul stopped the sermon, went down to the first floor where Eutychus was lying dead, and Paul fell on the dead body and gave the church assurance through the Holy Spirit that Eutychus was not dead but that his life was in him.

A miracle happened right then. Eutychus was brought back to life. I believe if anyone had doubted the power of God in the ministry and life of Paul, that would have ended the story. But instead, God used Paul to display his power.

The call of God comes with the power we have seen happen in the Scriptures. He called Moses and showed his presence with him. Elijah, Elisha, The three Hebrew boys, Esther, Daniel, Isaiah, Abraham, Jacob, Joseph, and the list goes on. Wherever you are, the presence of God must be seen and felt no matter what. "And let it be, when these signs come to you, that you do as the occasion demands; for God is with you." (I Samuel 10:7 KJV)

We will not have to struggle for his presence in any service if we prepare ourselves on our altar of prayer before coming forth. So do your best to ensure that you stay faithful to your call and leave no room to be questioned if God indeed called you. Shalom!

CHAPTER EIGHT

THE GOD MY PARENTS NEVER TOLD ME ABOUT

G rowing up to see my father and mother solely dedicated to the things of God was a blessing to me in that it opened many doors for me in my early stage. I watched my father pray for countless hours and still act as if he had just started praying. On many occasions, I always walk into my mom's room to find her on the floor with her black cover Bible and the church hymnbook. Her lips were moving, but I heard no sound. I would slowly and quietly walk out of the room to avoid interruption. A week will not go by without our church members coming to the house to spend the night in prayer. They will pray until you feel the house's foundation-shaking, sometimes till daybreak. My Dad and Mom did this almost every week, not minding that they had to wake up in the morning for another pre-scheduled church service.

I longed to be like Dad when it came to my prayer life. Nevertheless, there were many unanswered questions as a young boy watching from a close view. Despite all these prayers and fasting, things were happening to my parents, and I would have loved to step in and find a solution immediately. But Dad always said, "Let's leave it to God." I have never been able to comprehend this. In one of the stations my parents served, an Elder wrote a petition against my Dad and even went as far as calling him an occult member.

You may be inclined to believe that if you did not already know who my father was. Yes, I was of age at the time and was well aware of what was going on with my father, but he was unmoved by any of it. I would sit in the choir stand of the church, looking at him, smiling and shaking hands with the same people who wrote nasty things about him as if all had been settled. The only thing I could think of was, where is God in all this? Why is he not striking all these people dead by now? "This is the God my parents never told me about," I thought.

Why would he sit in heaven and watch some church Elders tarnish an innocent man this way? What is God doing about these things? So many questions were running through my mind, and no one could answer them. So finally, I concluded that God would not do anything about it, and it took him too long to get revenge.

I have been in the ministry for more than twenty years now, and despite those events, I frequently have to explain myself in front of the congregation. For example, in 2015, some group of persons wrote a six-page letter to our church in Nigeria and copied our home church here in Texas, claiming that I had fathered a child in Nigeria and I was a member of an occult group in Nigeria. They went as far as saying that the "Dad" ring my daughter gave me as a Father's Day gift was from the cult group. They wrote many things in that letter, but it took the grace of God for me not to quit church.

I quickly called my Dad, and I cried my eyes out that day. He told me, "Son, this is what ministry is about. Go and serve God. Do not bother yourself." He spoke to me about the things that will happen to any faithful gospel minister. When you carry the grace and anointing, you also have to expect persecution and hate.

I was furious, and I hated anything church during those times. I prayed as much as possible, but I wanted to investigate to know the writer of that letter and take matters into my own hands. In all of these things, God did not say anything at all, and may I also say here that during those times, God gave me the best sermons of all time in my entire ministry life and experience. I would preach in services, and people would be healed instantly, and things would happen that had never occurred in my religious background. I was shocked and sometimes speechless at the move of God. As much as I wanted those experiences, I longed for him to take revenge on those who penned those letters. I wished for the powers to make them blind, set fire to their houses, and maybe cripple them. In all honesty, I wanted this, but God had a different perspective. "Beloved, do not avenge yourselves, but rather give place to wrath; for it is written, "Vengeance is Mine, I will repay, says the Lord." (Romans 12:19 KJV)

My mentors, including my Dad, told me many things to expect in the ministry as a young preacher, but one thing they kept to themselves was that there would be moments and times when you call on God, and he says nothing. Not that he did not hear that prayer or heart cry, but he is waiting for an appointed and appropriate time. For those who do not have patience, this is where things fall apart. Unfortunately, as an active social media person, I see a lot of pastors falling victim to this.

They quickly come to social media platforms to defend themselves when accused of something. But, sometimes, they do more damage to the issue than solve it. This part of the ministry did not sit well, to begin with, but I had to roll with it. Knowing this part of God was calming and comforting.

Thus, it becomes clear why God allows particular circumstances in our life. Samson was ensnared in Deliliah's trap, yet God said nothing while it happened. God already knew John would be executed while incarcerated. Even though Jesus agonized on the cross for him, he said nothing, and the father of all creation did not intervene to save him. In contrast, the Bible says, *"Yet it pleased the Lord to bruise Him; He has put Him to grief. When You make His soul an offering for sin, He shall see His seed, He shall prolong His days, And the pleasure of the Lord shall prosper in His hand." (Isaiah 53:10 KJV)*

In the place of prayer, Jesus was tempted by the Devil, but he overcame them all. You will be drawn, ridiculed, talked about, accused in ministry, etc. Know that God will not leave you nor forsake you. During those difficult times in my life, I had one Scripture that kept me going. ..."For the Lord knows the way of the righteous, but the way of the ungodly shall perish." (Psalms 1:6 KJV)

Keep on doing the work of God; after all, nobody attacks an empty vessel. The enemy will only go after people with potential. I am confident that if my parents had told me this ahead of time, I would have been more prepared, but I sincerely believe they wanted me to explore this side of God on my own. It is sometimes painful to know that you, as a servant of God, will have to leave everything in the hands of God, including the ones you can solve right away if given a chance. Serving God is not easy!

The story of Joseph is a typical example of how God handles certain things in the life of a believer. Years ago, I preached on this Scripture in a virtual conference, and I tagged it "The Pit Experience." Joseph shared his dreams with his brothers, who would have prayed or fasted with him, but instead were envious of him, and his parents did not help matters. When you read the biblical account of Joseph, you will notice that one thing stands out: "God was with him." Despite Joseph's difficulties and suffering, God was always there, even when Potiphar's wife falsely accused him. However, Joseph refrained from intervening on his own. "But the Lord was with Joseph and showed him mercy, and He gave him favor in the sight of the prison keeper." (Genesis 39:21 KJV)

Let me challenge the young Ministers and Servants of God as you hold a copy of this book in your hands, know God for yourself. Have a personal experience with him. The God your father or mother served would not take you to heaven if you died in your sins. Neither will you go to heaven on your father or mother's credit or service before God. Impossible! My parents will never be able to teach me everything about God. I will need to know and explore some factors of God for myself. The same applies to my children. My duty as a father and their Pastor is to point them to and train them in the ways of God. Once they become adults, they must seek and know God for themselves. I am a firm believer in this Scripture, "Train up a child in the way he should go, And when he is old, he will not depart from it." (Proverbs 22:6 KJV)

You're furious with God because he did not do what you wanted him to do when you desired. God does not operate that way and will do what he said he would at the set time. Trying to prove a point when challenges arise is not the right way to operate, especially as a servant of God. I know it is difficult to say, but like my father told me, "Let God handle it." A thousand days before man is one day before God, and he will fight on your behalf.

The one person who wrote those false letters against me died a painful death after spending a lot of money in the hospital, and she finally confessed to what she did. I forgave her, which is another part of the ministry. It was pretty unfortunate that her end was something I would not wish on my worst enemy.

Back in my secondary school years, I had a senior prefect who hated me for no reason. I was not his agemate, but he would punish me anywhere he saw me and embarrass me in front of his colleagues. His friends warned him to leave me alone, but he would not listen to them. Because of this young man, my parents pulled me out of that school to avoid any more abuse from him.

Years later, I was invited to preach in a church in Nigeria. After the service, a young man in his early 40s ran out and knelt to greet me. I immediately told him to get up, and he proceeded to ask me if I recalled his face and I said no. He paused for about a minute and said, "I am Ephraim (Not his real name), your secondary schoolmate who used to flog you." Immediately, I had a flashback, and you could see anger and rage written on my face then. He could not look into my face anymore. With his head down, he whispered as softly as possible, "Sir, I am deeply sorry for all I did to you in school. My life has been a mess. Please pray for me." Honestly, I was a little hesitant, but the God in me had forgiven him right from that moment.

I embraced him in the parking lot and told him I had no ill feelings toward him. I prayed for him and gave him some money. He was so excited, and you could see him sigh in relief. In 2021, I was home to celebrate my Dad's new position in the church, and I saw him again. His countenance had changed. He was driving in a 2019 Toyota Camry, and God's presence was upon him. If I had wanted to retaliate back then in my school years, I probably wouldn't have been in that position to forgive or bless him. But God allowed me to go through those times. In return, he brought him before me like Joseph before his brothers, who could no longer recognize him.

Let God fight your battles; he knows how and when to do it. He will get the glory out of it, and you will be vindicated. If you are going through it now, remain calm and allow God to do his work. If you are yet to go through this phase of ministry, I pray that day never comes (it is not fun), but if you happen to go through it after, you must have read this book and be strengthened in the Lord. Let this Scripture be your guide. "And Moses said to the people, "Do not be afraid. Stand still and see the salvation of the Lord, which He will accomplish for you today. For the Egyptians you see today, you shall see again no more forever." (Exodus 14:13 KJV)

May God see you through!

CHAPTER NINE

HE IS A COVENANT KEEPER

L et me begin this chapter by saying that I am a living witness that God is a covenant-keeping God. I had every reason to believe my life was over when I traveled from Nigeria to The United States of America. I did not know anyone, cousins, friends, none whatsoever. I came solely by myself with my luggage. But God! God stood by me and with me, and I saw him move on my behalf from the moment I landed in America till date. It has been nothing but God. I mentioned in previous chapters that it is important to serve God without any strings attached, and when the time comes for God to reward you, you will see it happen without any stress.

Please permit me to share this story again here. Perhaps it will help and bless somebody who may be thinking about throwing in the towel. My Dad shared this story with me years ago, and it is still fresh in my mind. He said God had told him, "The Son I am giving you, if you guide and pray for him as much as you seek my face, I will use him for my glory, and it will surprise you."

A few years ago, while praying with my Dad in his living room with some prayer band members, the spirit of God passed through one of the men who came to pray with us and said the exact words. This time, I was of age to understand what God was saying because he spoke directly to me.

I started noticing those words coming to pass when I went for my visa appointment in 2002 with my Sister. Keep in mind that our appointments were for the same day and time. While my sister's visa application was turned down, mine was approved. Although I had been granted a visa, it was a sad day for us. Little did we realize that God had other plans. I left in 2003, flew to Oklahoma with a Landover in Chicago and an onward flight to Oklahoma City, and then the next day caught my flight to Amarillo, Texas. That was where the school van was going to pick me up for another two hours drive to Goodwell, Oklahoma.

Well, here is the breaking news. Since that was my first time flying overseas by myself with no one to help, when my flight landed in Chicago, I walked out of the flight, not knowing it was not my final destination. So instead, the plane left me in Chicago while waiting for my bags to arrive at the baggage claim.

I immediately called my Dad, and because of the time zone, I could not reach him, but thankfully, he had given me a list of people to call in case of an emergency. One of the persons I called was our church Deacon, Late Mr. Ernest Akpan, and he quickly jumped into action and helped me rebook a ticket to Oklahoma with Houston as my final destination. By this time, I was tired and ready to lie down. I flew into Oklahoma City that Sunday night at about 7 p.m. and waited for my flight to Houston at the terminal. I am not sure you are getting this twist so far. My ultimate intended destination was Amarillo, Texas, but God had another plan and sent me to Houston instead.

There I was received as a governor by one of our Pastors and his family, who would later become my spiritual father and in whose house I lived for four years. Two days after my arrival in the US, I boarded a flight to Amarillo, Texas, and I was received by our international relation agent, Linda Shoulders. From that moment, I saw the hands of God move on my behalf, from preaching in churches there to heading a youth department that was 100% white, and I was the only black person there. The handwriting of God was showing, and his covenant was manifesting. I believe that six years after I came to the US, my sister also went but this time around with her husband and three children. Look at what God has done.

Then she was unmarried and had no children, but God had a plan she did not see or know. Seasons are God's idea, and he will do what he promised at the right time and season. After my sophomore year in Oklahoma, I transferred to Houston to finish college. Even as the call of God began to manifest in my life, I saw him move in ways I could not understand. Favors upon favors, open doors, and many other things.

I have faced a lot of opposition in ministry, but what keeps me going is the covenant God made. "I will delight myself in Your statutes; I will not forget Your word." (Psalm 119:16 KJV)

You have no reason to worry when you have God in your corner. I would have been forgotten if not for God and his covenant upon my life. We have just recovered from one of the most dangerous diseases in the world. (Covid 19) This virus destroyed homes and closed churches, schools, mosques, and synagogues. There was little to no movement, and the land was dry. Some people lost their loved ones, and some were not allowed to attend the funeral of their loved ones.

It was a difficult time and year. But God! Despite all, God remembered his covenant in your life. Not that we are better than those who died, but God's covenant with you is that you will live and not die. "And as for Me, behold, I establish My covenant with you and with your descendants after you." (Genesis 9:9 KJV)

The God of covenant stands with you through the storm. Sometimes you lead while you are bleeding and feed others while you are hungry. Horatio Gates Spafford was a prominent American lawyer and Presbyterian church elder. He is best known for penning the famous Christian hymn, "It Is Well With My Soul." It Is Well With My Soul follows a family tragedy in which his four daughters died aboard the S.S. Ville du Havre on a transatlantic voyage.

When peace, like a river, attendeth my way,
When sorrows like sea billows roll;

Whatever my lot, Thou hast taught me to say,

It is well. It is well with my soul.

I believe God is a covenant keeper and a source of inspiration at my worst moments. God judges motive before he judges action. So have this in your mind: no matter the circumstance, he will never fail in his word. The God who called you will always show up for you. We cannot go by how we feel. We must go by God's word, which is his covenant with us. Nobody gets to pick the battles they will have to fight or families they will have to be born into, so the fight you find yourself in today or the things going on in your life today was carefully orchestrated by God even before you were born. The greatest battles in life are assigned to strong men and women. God would not allow you to go through this phase if he did not have faith in you. "Being confident of this very thing, that he which hath begun a good work in you will perform it until the day of Jesus Christ." (Philippians 1:6 KJV)

When it is painful, do not get discouraged. Get ready; you are about to give birth. That discomfort you feel it's not just a random pain; it is birth pain. There is a gift in that pain. There is a new level in that pain. Please do not waste it. Look for opportunities and praise God through them.

Hear me: "Your problems will drain you, but you will not drown."

God will take you places you did not dream of, and he will be there with you. Sometimes you will feel alone but remember he will never leave or forsake you. I have many instances that speak to this. I have seen him do it, heal a cripple person, open the eyes of the blind, restore people to health, and many other things. That same God who brought me through the many storms in my life and was the pilot that flew my plane and stirred the boat of my life will keep you lest you fall. He will be with you, sustain you amid your lack, raise men to support and help you, and walk with you in the dark times and days. He will never forsake you. Every minister must bear this cross; therefore, if you haven't yet encountered this phase of ministry, I am praying for you. Know this and have it in your heart that our God is a covenant keeper and will never fail.

CHAPTER TEN

THE VOICE OF GOD

The voice of God is not of Man! I believe that we have turned the voice of God into the voice of Man in this century. We want to listen more to what Man says versus what God says. In February of 2021, I flew to Dallas, Texas, to surprise and support a brother in the ministry. When I got there, he was running two services, and I decided to stay through the whole service. After the first service, he had a brief meeting while I took that time to glance through the city and some food places. After his session, he called me into his office. He whispered, "Apostle, God wants you to speak to his people in the second service." I was shocked, not because I had nothing to preach about or was shy to speak, but because I had heard God say to me, "Son, prepare to speak," so I prepared what I would say should he call me to preach. God pointed me to this Scripture, "And the people gave a shout, saying, It is the voice of a God, and not of a man." (Acts 12:22 KJV)

Right there and then, I was carried away in the spirit, and the Lord began to minister to me in that service before I mounted the pulpit. He said, "Tell my people I am still speaking at this age." Our generation is running after prophecies and miracles while God is still speaking. If you pause and read your word, you will know that God is still speaking and has been speaking. Hungry men and women are opening churches in the name of "God called me." Yet, the things you see and hear do not align with what the God of Heaven would send anyone to do on his behalf. The abomination that is going on in today's church has got me wondering if they have any fear of God inside of them.

A man of God told me in New York that I should raise an offering once I am done preaching. I asked him why. He smiled and said, "Pastor, we have to settle your hotel bill and honorarium." I was so upset that he saw the revival as a money-making scheme to milk the people of God, not minding if they had it. He was not concerned about their souls; he only wanted to get money from them. He never stopped to think if that was the will of God. The Bible clearly says the angel of God smote him (killed him) because he did not give glory to God. We have taken the glory of God in his church because he is a merciful God. We tend to think He no longer kills or destroys.

In today's world, men and women have no fear of God because they know what they are saying is not from God, but they have no guilty conscience, so it does not bother them. Some put charms in their eyes, mouth, and pockets; some even swallow them for power and

56

relevance. My prayer is, may God have mercy on this generation's ministers. We need to go back to the old-time religion where men and women of God slept in the church, seeking the presence of God for real.

There is a birth ready to occur in the body of Christ, where people will hear and see the real presence of God. The voice of God is necessary for this generation, and I dare not move until I listen to God's voice and not Man's. If we spend time before God, we will hear what God has to say to his children. We have magnified the voice of Man immensely, and it has destroyed many of our people. It is time to seek the sound of heaven, the voice of God. We must learn to identify when God speaks and when the flesh is at work.

We each must seek the face of God to know if, indeed, the spirit that is speaking is of God. The familiarity of the speaking spirit should not carry us away because of our situations. When faced with an unpleasant condition that needs an immediate solution, we can be fooled by a spirit seemingly offering a solution that is not of God. Remember that Satan also became an angel of light **(II Corinthians 11:14 KJV).** As a believer in Christ, guard your heart and also your spirit. You will learn to filter things for yourself by seeking God's kingdom and believing that God would add everything else to you. **(Mathew 6:33 KJV).**

Zedekiah, the Son of Kenaanah, made iron horns and declared that the Lord had spoken through him to the king in winning the war with the Arameans. That was not the voice of God; that was the voice of Man.

"And all the prophets prophesied, saying, Go up to Ramothgilead, and prosper: for the LORD shall deliver it into the king's hand. And the messenger that was gone to call Micaiah spake unto him, saying, Behold now, the words of the prophets declare good unto the king with one mouth: let thy word, I pray thee, be like the word of one of them and speak that which is good. And Micaiah said, As the LORD liveth, what the LORD said unto me, that will I speak." (I Kings 22:11-12)

Micaiah, who heard directly from God, had already prepared himself to speak what God showed to him. This perfectly illustrates how to act as men and women of God. Do not be afraid to speak up. Micaiah said what God told him to say directly before the king with no fear. Bear in mind that he stood before the king, knowing very well that his life was in the hands of the king. Even after all other Prophets spoke with one accord, he made it known that he would only say what God had shown to him and directed him to say to the king. The audacity and authority to speak to anyone come from God. Be bold! Be fearless! Be firm!

When you read I Kings chapter 22 further, you will notice that the King sent for Micaiah, not the other way round. Nowadays, men and women of God are in politics and the government's pockets, which is why they cannot hear when God is speaking. There used to be a time when the government sought after ministers to listen to what God was saying to them. I love Micaiah's reply, *"As the Lord Liveth,"* he centered everything on God, not the king's pocket or influence. God First!

How many of us today can look into the eyes of the President, governor, mayor, or any politician and tell them the bitter truth? Careless if it hurts, or will you ever be invited to speak, preach or repeat a prayer? Do not do anything to please men or look good before them. Let all you do be to the glory of God and nothing else. Let the whole world hate you; as long as God loves you, that is all that matters. Take a look at what the King says to Micaiah, *"And the king said unto him, How many times shall I adjure thee that thou tell me nothing but that which is true in the name of the Lord?" (1 Kings 22:16 KJV)*

Even the King knew that Micaiah was speaking the mind of God, and he challenged him to say what God had shown to him. Finally, the heavens opened, and Micaiah, already prepared and ready to speak, went wild with the word. After he had declared what God showed to him, he was punished by the King. Sometimes there will be consequences for standing by the truth. People will hate you for speaking the mind of God. "And Micaiah said, If thou return at all in peace, the LORD hath not spoken by me. And he said, Hearken, O people, every one of you." (1 Kings 22:28 KJV)

Look at the boldness of this Prophet. He was sound and bold enough to face the king, not minding what would happen. If you return in peace, then know that God did not speak through me. This generation needs godly men and women of this kind. Regardless of the season and time, people will come to you for sound wisdom because you hear directly from God, and when you speak, heaven honors you. So let us go back to the roots and passion we once had for the things of God. Stand on the truth, seek his glory and his presence. Remember, To Be Publicly Powerful, You Must be Privately Prayerful.

CHAPTER ELEVEN

A GENERATION OF NOISEMAKERS

It is painful, but permit me to single this particular topic out how I want to. I am not being personal here, nor am I being selective, but I will love to speak in a broad term. When I see things happening in our churches, I ask myself hard questions. By the grace of God, I have been privileged to worship in a different congregation other than my birth church.

I may be Pentecostal, but I love to worship God with people from other denominations. Unfortunately, I see a prevalent thing in our churches nowadays, where preachers will get up and tell the congregation to speak in tongues, not minding if there is anyone in the building who may be a first-timer, stranger, guest, Muslim, etc. I know what you are thinking as you are reading this line. You are probably saying they are not speaking to Man but God. I get that part, but the critical thing here is that demons can speak in tongues too. It will be challenging and almost impossible for anyone watching others say in languages they do not understand not to mimic what they hear or see just to fit in. "But as he which hath called you is holy, so be ye holy in all manner of conversation." (I Peter 1:15 KJV)

How can you say you are filled with the Holy Spirit yet cannot make a sentence without cursing or using vain language? When the spirit of God is in you, he takes over you and everything in you. The spirit of God changes you from your old self to your new self. You cannot be saved and filled with the Holy Spirit and still live the life you used to live. This is what we call true transformation. Most pastors are struggling with their sexual life. In the morning, they are Pastors, but at night they become willy-nelly. Some struggle with drugs, and some are sex offenders in disguise.

Years ago in Houston, a Catholic Bishop had just finished preaching a powerful sermon to his congregation. That same Saturday night, he was spotted in a strip club pinning money on women. The news was everywhere, and his people hardly believed it. If you saw him on stage, you would be tempted to kiss his feet because he was good, but he had a secret life that many did not know. He spoke in tongues, I would assume it was the Holy Spirit, and anyone would have been caught up in believing that he had just met with God seeing him minister with such passion on the pulpit. He was just a noisemaker.

What kind of sound are you producing?

On the altar, many pastors can preach and use fancy words, yet not one life is saved. Some people can speak in tongues today and tomorrow, yet they are depraved on the inside. Do you know that demons, too, can speak in tongues? There are noises everywhere, in almost all the streets and cities, but things are yet to change. If we profess God the way we do in our churches, we should be able to see the changes in our community and society as well. But the noises only end inside the church building. Some do not pray at home, while others try to spend at least a minute or two hoping they do not fall asleep. Our churches are filled with noisemakers but have nothing to show for in ministry. Many preachers are operating with the spirit of witchcraft in the house of God. If we have the real Holy Spirit, this will be a thing of the past.

Anytime you contact somebody who has received the Holy Spirit for real, you will attest that God is in them, yet most preachers will mount the pulpit knowing they have just finished indulging in a sexual act with an outsider who is not their wife or husband. Where is the fear of God in all of this? They make the loudest noise, yet no ounce of spirituality in them.

Speaking in tongues does not mean you have the holy spirit of God inside of you. That you are a prayer band member, singer, and instrumentalist makes no difference nowadays to some people. For example, I recently saw a video where a church choir leader was sexually dancing behind a naked lady in the club, and the following day he was on stage leading in worship. I want you to understand me here, and I did not say that when you have the holy spirit, you should not go out with friends anymore, eat out, or visit the unbelievers anymore. I am saying that there are certain things the holy spirit will say NO to, regardless of how you try to fight them. "What? Know ye not that your body is the temple of the Holy Ghost which is in you, which ye have of God, and ye are not your own?" *(I Corinthians 6:19 KJV)*

Ministers, church workers, and members must go back to the basics of what was laid down as the church's guiding principles, which is the body of Christ. I long for those days when people came to church solely to hear from God, not because the pastor, brother, or sister was there. I long for those days when our ministers allow God to take charge of his church.

I look forward to that day when our choirs will minister under the unction of the spirit of God. Recently, I got a video clip on my WhatsApp sent to me by one of our Elders in the church.

This video showed a spirit-filled choir ministering, and the spirit of God swept through them. Some could not stand to sing, while some were soaked in tears as they ministered. These are the days we long to see in the church again. We are tired of the watered-down system introduced into the church; we all know this is not God. We know it is coming from the pits of hell.

In one of our prayer sessions in church, after two hours of counseling and prayers for the out-of-town guest. I dragged myself to the car with my family. As I started the engine of the vehicle to pull out of the parking lot, our six-year son, who had witnessed all the miracles and prayers God had used me to do in the church, said to me, "Dad, I want the holy spirit" my ears popped open. I asked him, "Son, what did you say?" He looked into my rare view mirror from his car seat and whispered, "I need the holy spirit." Right there and then, I stepped out of the car, took him inside the church, and began to pray for him. I laid my hands on him, asking the Lord to baptize him with the gift of the holy spirit.

We need to live in a generation where both men and women thirst for the things of God. No crowds, fame, or luxurious lifestyle, but all they want is the presence of God and the holy spirit. The holy spirit will silence every other voice and noise in the church because he is the only authentic voice we know.

He will speak the truth to our ears. He will direct the affairs of the church and will never lead us astray. Let me add this: *please do not claim that God informed you if you did not hear from him.* In the ministry of today, this is what has dispersed and destroyed many congregations. Many have become victims because they wanted to "hear" God by all means, so they have been lied to in the name of God. Return to Bethel, that place of prayer, and watch God do wonder. Let me share an experience here so this will stick in your mind as you read this book. I attended our annual church convention in Nigeria in 2017, where the Lord spoke through a Prophetic message saying there would be a significant disease and many people, even believers, would lose their lives. Fast forward to November 2019, two years after that prophecy, the first-ever recorded case of covid hit. Many people died, and all the countries in the world were affected. The person God used to give that prophecy is still alive today, and indeed, we can attest to the fact that he heard directly from God.

Having God's spirit is vital in today's church, seeing the vast majority of doctrines in our churches. We need the holy spirit. The holy spirit will direct the affairs of the church, and flesh will not be able to dominate. Our pastors, church workers, choir members, protocol team, and all components that make up the church administration must be willing to submit to the leadership of the holy spirit. Any church that is run in the flesh can never stand. Gone are the days when we used to quote Scriptures, say a couple of prayers, and then call it a day. Today's church needs teaching and prayers. No man or woman can accomplish this without the leadership of the holy spirit. The people will know when we start operating in the spirit. Let us not be led by sentiments and flesh but submit to the leadership of the holy spirit.

My late Uncle told me a story of how the Holy Spirit kept him away from boarding a plane to Cameroon. He had a revelation of a plane crash while asleep. He woke up and started praying then God told him not to travel. As stubborn as he was, I would assume, he went to the airport, and the first sign that God showed him was him misplacing his identification card. After then, he kept hearing a voice urging him to return home, but he refused to obey. Finally, just before boarding the aircraft, God made his bladder so full that he could not keep it back any longer, so he had to visit the bathroom.

He had to do the number two at the restroom, and it was almost like he had diarrhea. He tried getting up to clean himself but could not because it was uncontrollable. Like other airports and flight policies, the gate agent closed the doors after everyone boarded, and it was too late when he rushed to board the plane. Upset and frustrated at everyone at the terminal, he walked away and took a taxi home after rebooking the flight for the next day. At about 9 p.m. that evening, he heard the news on his radio that there was a plane crash. He hurried over to his neighbor's house, which at the time had a television. To his utmost surprise, he discovered that it was the plane he was about to board, which he missed while using the restroom. Tears rolled down his face as he began to worship God right inside his neighbor's living room. He shared the story of what had happened before the plane crash. The following is not a movie script. It did take place. It was the Holy Spirit that saved him that day. The Holy Spirit is a compass, and if you pay attention to him, you will never regret the pathway he will take you through.

As ministers of God, this is what we need the most in our churches - *The Holy Spirit.* The absence of the Holy Spirit makes ministers of God entertain instead of admonishing. I am trusting God for a great move and change to take place in our churches and communities. Then and only then will we experience the real presence of God through the work of the holy spirit. Stop the noise so we can hear a sound from heaven.

CHAPTER TWELVE

BE GUIDED AND GUARDED

s a minister, you must allow the Spirit of God to guide you in all you set out to do to advance the kingdom of God. You must have certain reservations in your actions by staying guarded in your actions and reactions, careful not to fall victim to the wimps and caprices of the crowd who applaud your every move as you serve. In my walk with God and for God, I learned early in ministry that the masses will fool you with their applause and noise. Some will come because they have heard so much about you, some because they know you personally, and some claim to support you.

As a minister, you must be guarded. The people God will send to you may turn out to be the old, young, poor, and less privileged, and you have to be ready to embrace all with love in your heart. The people God sends to you first may have very little to offer you in terms of financial support, which is much needed at the beginning of the church but do not be discouraged; know this truth that this is always the beginning of every true church.

There will be a little storm in the beginning, but once the church takes off, you will see the glory of God manifesting in it. Many ministers get carried away at the beginning, and when those who came because of what they heard finally leave, they become frustrated and start blaming the enemy for it. Do not allow the crowd to get you out of character or make you think everyone is for you.

Allow me to bring to life my experience of being guided and guarded. Some years back, I was invited to a five-day conference in Florida and was one of the guest speakers. While I was ministering, a young lady was in front of me, taking notes as if I were selling some magic skin lotion. As I rounded up and moved into a brief worship session, she was in tears, and the Lord ministered to me about some of the things she was going through.

I knew right there I was in something new, so immediately after service, I called her into the Pastor's office and delivered the message from God to her. She told me how her husband had died inside the church. Tears would not allow her to speak freely. Her two years old son clung to her arms. She looked at me and said, "Pastor, my husband used to be a minister, and he would counsel people from morning till dawn, pray for them and listen to their needs, but most of them were not our members." At that moment, I had a flashback to when I was a child watching my Dad talk to people day in and day out from morning until dawn; sometimes, we had to take food to him at the church because he had so many people trying to seek his counsel that he would not have time to take a break or get out from his church office.

The young mother lamented in the church office as I sat soaked in my suit from two and a half hours of preaching. I thought to myself, "this could have been me" she went into the details of how her husband would fast from Monday to Friday with barely anything in his system besides water; all he wanted to see was the church being filled up to the brim. Finally, she mentioned that she had tried so many times to tell him that it was a gradual process, but he did not have the patience to wait on God.

He was disheartened after each service since the church was barely empty. People came to pray because he was talented at it, but none of them wanted to become members. He passed away when he should not have. The thought of getting his church filled to the brim was all he wanted. I honestly had no words at that point to say to her as a word of comfort, but I prayed for her and her baby and gave her the little token I had. Not to mention that the church was closed down after the death of her husband.

We must be guided and guarded on our desires for the church we want to see versus the church God wants to build through us. I know of a church in Houston where many people go once a year because the pastor there gets to bring other celebrity pastors there for two to three nights. That is the only time you will see that church open.

The critical question Is, "Should the crowd move us?" Are we after the crowd or the crown? One of the

71

things I pride myself in is that when God gives me a message, I do not wait until I am in front of a big crowd to deliver it. I do not care about the size of the public, and I will preach as though I am preaching in a Benny Hinn crusade. Yet, in that same crowd, there are people for whom God has prepared that message, and they are there for a reason to receive it at that particular time.

Take note of this, "The right crowd will come when you deliver the message to the right people."

Many are where they are today because they placed too many expectations on people who were only interested in "stopping by" but not "belonging."

Many say, "I am only going there to support him." Ministry is not a business, and it is only a business you go to support. The Ministry world is a place where iron sharpens iron. We do everything together because it is an Apostolic journey. When I am invited to speak in other churches, I arrive there early, and if there is anything to do to help in the setup, I join in and get it done. Countless times, I have had to help the Pastor, and his family arrange the church, connect the keyboard, set up chairs, etc. But that did not take the glory from me as the guest minister. Instead, I received my blessings from God there and then.

As a Pastor, you must be able to separate pleasure from ministry. Play when it is the right time to play and be serious when it is time to be serious. Do not give yourself away to vain things, or else you will be used as a rag. I have seen many preachers start well, and suddenly, they fall because they failed to be guided and guarded.

Emotion is another killer of the brethren. Maybe you did not read that well. Let me repeat it. EMOTION is one of the killer diseases that most ministers cannot get rid of. Yes, we can preach to make somebody happy and bring the roof down, but the rest becomes a story for another day when we step off that pulpit. Many ministers preach from a place of unforgiveness, bitterness, and hate. They will quote Scriptures of what you need to do to be forgiven by God, but they are not on talking terms with their spouses at home. Some do not sleep on the same bed. To be guided and guarded, you must forgive and heal before preaching forgiveness.

This goes back to what I mentioned earlier in chapter 9 of this book. Ministers are cross-bearers and, as such, must be guarded and guided. My Father once asked me a question when I approached him about some things I was facing in the ministry as a young man; He looked at me and smiled as usual, and then the next thing he did was to clear his throat, which was a sign that he had something to say in response. "Son, who do you look up to in life as a Pastor?" That was an unexpected question, and immediately I said, "Dad and Bishop TD Jakes." He was probably trying to put me to the test since I think he already knew the answer. He said that no matter how intelligent a person may be, they must have somebody they love and look up to in life and ministry. Somebody who will guide and guard them no matter what.

No matter how complex your circumstances or emotions may be, this is the person you will pay attention to. When this one individual talks to you, it will diffuse your anger. I drew my energy from this conversation with my father while he was still speaking with me. I knew that a day would come when I would have to reach out to my mentor or spiritual father for some advice or guidance, and that could not just be any man.

In today's gospel ministry, the word "Spiritual Father" has been deeply abused and watered to a scope of little or no value. Many ministers do not take that word seriously more than a typical relationship or a cliché. It has become a clique. You can never get to the top without having somebody who will guide and guard you. Moses needed Joshua, Elijah and Elisha, David and Jonathan, Esther and Mordecai, Pharaoh and Joseph, God and Abraham, Naomi and Ruth, and this list of Biblical examples is inexhaustible.

Looking closely into these relationships, you will see their role in making each other great; some went as far as impacting powers. I always question those who say they are veterans in the gospel ministry as if they had no one to guide or guard them. As a young minister, know this truth, no man is an island, regardless of where you will find yourself tomorrow. The above is valid not just for the church but also for the corporate and governmental worlds. Never assume that you know it all just because you attended a theological school, for learning is an everyday process. You will need somebody in your life to guard and guide you besides God. Realize that you will make mistakes in life and ministry but do not dwell upon them.

There is much work to do to get the church ready for the return of Jesus Christ, so we fall, but we must get up to run the race set before us, winning souls for the Kingdom of our Father. Be guided and guarded at all times by putting on the complete armor of God. "Put on the whole armor of God, that ye may be able to stand against the wiles of the Devil." (Ephesians 6:11 KJV)

As a conscientious person, I have lived and maintained one philosophy: I always ask questions where my strength and knowledge fail. But on the other hand, some ministers feel they do not need anyone to get to the top. Some are boastful, and some are filled with uncircumcised pride. Many of them despise being reprimanded, and because of their pride and belief that they have reached the pinnacle of ministry, they miss God and His instructions in season, causing them to die before their time.

As a gospel minister, you must realize that you cannot arrive at the zenith while living on earth. Our zenith arrival is when we run the race before us well and gain our crown and rightful position in eternity with Jesus Christ. Only then can we genuinely arrive. No matter the accolades, the applause we receive, the cheering and compliments as we serve in the vineyard of our Lord, He wants us to be alert and guided at all times. Moses had this experience when God said to him, "My presence will go with you." God went before him and showed out before the Egyptians, even before those who thought they were strong. "And he said, My presence shall go with thee, and I will give thee rest." (Exodus 33:14 KJV)

When he speaks about "REST," you have no reason to worry about anything. This is why David declares boldly, "I will fear no evil." On the other hand, when guided and guarded by God, you become a terror in the enemy's camp. I had an experience some years ago in Haiti while I was there for a four days revival. I stayed in the Pastor's mission house, and some police security and gatemen guarded me. At about 2:28 am, I was awake because it was hot, and there was no AC or fan to cool the room. I saw a woman's shadow with a tail and long hair walking inside my room, and immediately I sat up and began to pray, hoping that it would move from where it stood. Thirty minutes later, I saw flames and smoke coming in from the living room area, and all I could do was call on Jesus that morning. When the Pastor came in the morning to check on me, he mentioned that there had been so much movement in the house, but that night he did not hear or notice any movement. I thanked the Lord that day because I knew God had sent his angels, and I was well protected. One of my favorite Bible verses is this: *"Except the LORD build the house, they labor in vain that build it: except the LORD keep the city, the watchman waketh but in vain." (Psalm 127:1 KJV)*

You must believe that as God's servant, his presence is constantly with you to direct all you do. When you are without his presence, you act by the flesh and are reminded that God's gift is undeserved, but his company will take something from you while keeping you functioning in Adam's manner.

I am not a fan of American football, but something drew my attention to it so much that I almost cannot miss it for anything whenever the season starts. The football coach stands at the sideline with a headset connected to his quarterback, the key player and playmaker on the field. So when he calls a play, his quarterback and the players can hear. Yet, again, since the quarterback is the eyes of the game, he gets to see and know how the other team will react to that particular play and has the power to change the play, knowing full well that he may fumble or make a touchdown on that specific play.

That is the same way God treats us—we are the coach, and he is the quarterback with authority to alter the play at any time. As a result, he protects us from making poor decisions in life, and occasionally when He notices that what we are ordering on the field will not be in our favor, He steps in and quickly changes to protect us from the enemy. "The LORD orders the steps of a good man: and he delighteth in his way." (Psalms 37:23 KJV)

The keyword there is "STEPS." May I also point out that he will order your STEPS and STOPS? WOW! That's some good stuff right there. Let this sink into your spirit. Anyone who God genuinely calls must be guided and guarded by the word of God and nothing else. May your prayer be, "O Lord, order my steps in your way and guide me in making decisions that will be pleasing to you." Amen!

Our decision must be pleasing God as He orders our steps daily to live a guided and guarded life, bringing Him glory and honor.

CHAPTER THIRTEEN

DROPPED BUT NOT DAMAGED

T oo often, we have seen and heard of ministers who have committed suicide, some struggling with drugs, and some who cannot get rid of their old selves. In so many instances, I have counseled ministers who were too shy or ashamed to come clean about who they were in real life.

Most experienced maltreatment as children and did not get along well with their parents. The apparent explanation for these problems is that they were dropped and some of them were damaged. I preached this theme in a sermon I delivered some time ago. One thing that rings in my mind when I see ministers who struggle with one issue or the other is when healing will happen for them. You cannot preach or minister when you are hurting or have been abused.

You cannot minister until you have been administered. God is not an author of confusion and wants his house to be clean. How can you speak of healing when you have been hurt? Hurt people hurt others. You cannot bleed and try to stop others from bleeding. Impossible!

Ministering from a place of hurt cannot take the church of God anywhere. *Nowadays, we have gays and lesbians leading the choir, and the church is jumping up and down and getting entertained.* Something has to change in the body of Christ. Most preachers are suffering inside, and nobody is helping them; some have infirmities they cannot tell anyone about. Some have died in their place of duty because they did not take out time to heal from their sickness. I know of a Minister who died on the pulpit because he did not listen to the doctor's order. Yes, God is the one who gives us good health, but he has also given us doctors and nurses to take care of us.

Do not tempt God. Know when to draw a line and put an end to some things when that time comes. Please stop trying to entertain people when it is time to end it. Many ministers are dying every day because they overdid themselves. Running revivals after revivals, conferences here and there, and a very crowded traveling itinerary to make themselves look big. There is no time to rest, but the Bible states that God rested on the seventh day. When I see pastors depriving themselves of rest, I am left with one question: When will they sleep?

The lack of rest and self-care has caused many of our ministers pain and a never-ending bruise. You have been dropped. Drop from the man who molested you, the father who abused you, the mother who cursed you, the uncle who called you names, cousins who never wanted to deal with you in any form or shape, and many others.

This experience lingered in your mind and heart that it has affected your preaching, and you cannot recover from the pain. You can only truly heal from the pains of wrong done to you by dropping the damage and riding ahead with Christ, who conquered it all through His pains to be hung on the cross for you and me. Set your house in order, and that includes your health. God wants to do something with you, and he wants you to be whole and healed, but how can you achieve this when you have been dropped?

My Pastor in Oklahoma once shared with me some profound things he experienced in school. He was raped and abused by his uncle. His Father and Mother did not believe it, and it took him years to open up about it. He was preaching and making waves, yet inside of him, he was dropped. Finally, one day he decided to confront his uncle about everything that happened to him. He forgave him, prayed for him, and let everything go. I am so glad he did that before he breathed his last. Forgiveness is a crucial component in our love work with God. The forgiveness we offer to those who have trespassed against us gives us a spot on the table with Jesus Christ. If you want to remain relevant to God and not be dropped, you must be like God and master the act of forgiveness. Unfortunately, some ministers are operating from a deep place of hurt.

I knew a young minister in the church in his early 40s, the young man had the word and was a gifted minister in music as well, but he had a problem. He was struggling with his sexuality. The young man came to me one day to confide in me because he could no longer keep it to himself. I had to ask him, "What are you not telling me?" Have you been struggling with your sexuality while ministering before the saints? I asked him why he was comfortable talking to me about it. He responded, "because you will not judge me, and you have the heart filled with Godly love to encourage me with a word in the season as you possess the mouth that is like the pen of a ready writer." If we leave sentiments out and deal with the actual essence of what we are going through, we will be able to heal from the inside out.

I believe God is a healer, and I know him to be one. But he has also given us the will to know that if one is having pain, it is reasonable to take some pain medication and probably rest, and such a person will recover. Famous gospel ministers have been dropped, and some never forgave the man or woman who abused them, yet they are comfortable preaching about abuse and forgiveness to their members. I cannot attest to the validity of this story; still, a well-known pastor in America died some years ago inside a hotel room, and the hotel manager found a rolled-up paper of marijuana in his pocket.

It was a shame to hear what happened to that Man of God. Some said it was a setup by the police officers who were the first responders, and some said he was addicted to cocaine. Nobody knew this except for the pastor and his God. It was something he was struggling with while preaching "Sin no more" to his congregation. In our African culture, this is so often that when a young person is mistreated or raped, no one wants to talk about it and instead tries to keep the victim quiet as much as possible. These are all giants we have as an epidemic sour in the body of Christ.

Dropped but not damaged means you will go through the wilderness where you will encounter giants of life like sickness, financial struggles, hate, rejections, blackmail, and scratches on your faith. Oh my, your patience will be tried by those you love the most. Understand that every experience in life is to bring you to a place of closeness with God. The scratches are your sage of honor, so you must wear them with a revelation that God will not allow the drop to damage you, and you deserve the harvest for not being weary in doing good. If you have been dropped, get back up and learn how to walk again, get back up and leap again, and start afresh. I know you were dropped but thank God you were never damaged. Live again!

CHAPTER FOURTEEN
IT IS UNDER CONTROL

T he wind stood still and obeyed Him. The sun stood still until Moses won the battle with the children of Israel. He divided The Red Sea with only his rod, as instructed by God. The rod of Moses budded, and it turned into a snake and swallowed all of the chief priests of Egypt right in front of their Pharaoh. All these historical biblical events occurred to showcase God's sovereignty-**CONTROL's supremacy.** Sarah could have borne a child for Abraham before menopause, but God was in control of that not happening at the time they wanted. Come with me; let us take a journey through situations of life. We all go through it, and no one is exempted from the trials and temptations that befall a man. Whatever that situation is, IT IS UNDER CONTROL.

He says, "Be still, and know that I am God; I will be exalted among the nations, ; I will be exalted in the earth." (Psalm 46: 10 KJV)

This Scripture brings me so much comfort and

peace whenever I read it, and I am sharing it with you as I pen down this chapter. If you read it slowly to retain the authenticity of God's assuring love for you, you will understand that this is God himself speaking to you in this passage of the Bible. Thus, with assurance and in the name of Jesus, I am telling you that whatever is troubling you and making you lose sleep, "IT IS UNDER CONTROL." Therefore, be still and know that God is in charge of your existence on earth, and you should trust him to understand what He is doing.

As we grow older in life, our bodies begin to transition and depending on how we treat our bodies while young, things start to change. Have you been to the doctor, and the lab results brought you to a state of regret wishing you had paid more attention to your health? The medical report has got you panicking, and you are losing sleep? God has it under control. Is the rent due? Are bills past due? Are you in a place of little or no love? Are you confused about the decision you have to make but do not know what to do? Are you feeling rejected? Do you think people will mock you if God does not show up? Take a chill pill, for it is written, "I will never leave you nor forsake you." IT IS UNDER CONTROL.

I have dealt with so much in life that there was a time I had no clue where school fees would come from, and I risked being dropped out of the university. I quit school several times, but today, the Lord has used me to write this message in this book to be an encouragement to you that it is under control. I have a conviction in my spirit that nothing will turn you down, nothing that will make you cry, and nothing that will make you put your hands on your head and say, "Had I known!"

They have laughed at you for too long, but God has stepped in your matter; therefore, there is nothing that will make people ask you, "where is your God?" God is sending me to tell you that it does not matter how long it has been, how many things you have done to get to the finish line but failed, or what people say. God is saying now to you with assurance; I have it under control. Therefore, you must be still and know He is always with you.

The world's economy has collapsed, and we are risking more because Timothy already warned us in his book that critical times are hard to deal with. We live in critical days where men are lovers of themselves rather than God. Men are unfeeling, unkind, and self-centered. In this crucial moment, I know you are praying and needing answers from the Lord. Sometimes, it seems God has forgotten you, and the answers to your prayers tarry; do not give up! So many times, we forget that Jesus is in the boat. Just like He was in the boat with Peter and the other disciples, they had no idea that the owner of the universe was also in the boat, and He had all powers to silence anything. Too many times, we rush to conclusions without knowing that God has it under control. The vision is plain and though it tarries, wait for its manifestation.

I write as one with a pen of a ready writer and with an Apostolic mandate. I decree: whatever you place before the Lord, be still, be confident in Him as He says to you, "I know the thought and pain that you have in your heart; I know what you are facing." I understand the condition of your neighborhood. I am aware of the status of your marriage, I am aware of the difficulties you are experiencing at school, and I am aware that your business is faltering. I am aware of what you are going through among your peers in the church and the struggles of your relationship, and I am aware of who is talking about you, laughing at you, pointing fingers at you, and mocking you. It has been brought under control.

So many times, we seem not to understand the God we serve. Sometimes, it is just as though we are wrestling not with the fact that this God can do anything but we wrestle with the fact that He is the same God who did the things that we read about Him in the Scripture. The Bible says He parted the red sea. That is the same God we are talking about. He will never change. Men may vary, but God will never change. The Bible says He is the same yesterday, today, and forever. He said, " The stone the builders rejected would be the chief cornerstone." Now, let me ask you this: Is anybody going to love you like you deserve to be loved? Is there anybody who is going to care for you? Is there anybody better than Him?

He knows the end from the beginning. He knows every hair on your head. The Lord who created you understands and knows where you are heading. There is absolutely nothing that God does not know. And as you read this book, He also whispers in your ear that He has it under control.

I may not know what the hit is or what it is that you want Him to put under control. I do not know who restricts you from being all God has called you to be, nor do I know what opposes God's glory in your life. I am not sure what's been upsetting you, causing you to lay in bed but unable to sleep. I am not sure what has led you to believe that your life is finished and that nothing can be restored, but I write as a servant and a vessel of God to tell you that the Lord stated He has it under control, for nothing is too hard for him to do.

The Bible says, "For I know the thoughts I have about you; it is the thought of peace and not of war to give you an expected end." (Jeremiah 29:11 KJV)

According to the Bible text above, God knows what is best for you and what will work in your favor. As a result, God knows what to do to make you happy. So He says, "I know what you're going through. Be not afraid, for I have it under control."

Maybe you are going through pain, and you prayed, took medication, and did all you could; nothing is changing. I want you to know that God has it under control. Do you know how excited I am sitting here writing that God has it under control? Do you know what that means? Do you see the power in the word "God has it under control"? The Bible says He was in the ship and was sleeping, and there came a tempest of the storm raging, and the disciples asked, *"carest not that we perish?"* Do you not care that we shall perish while you lie here sleeping and snoring? Does it not bother you? They had no idea that the Lord of Lords and the King of Kings had the power to rebuke the ocean.

When Jesus is in the boat, it does not matter the storm. It makes no difference what people say about you or whether they point fingers at you. When Jesus is in your boat, you will give birth to that child. When Jesus is in your boat, you will get healthy and explore financially. When Jesus is in your boat, your marriage will be perfect. When Jesus is in your boat, everything is under control.

The idea of people who understand God is confusing here because many think that when God is silent, He does not care, but the reverse is the case. When He is silent on your situation, that is when He is working the most for you. He is trying to tell you that He is in control and will bring answers to your problems. He will obtain the result and make it beautiful that those who were talking about you, laughing at you, and pointing fingers would come back and ask, "What did you do?" What sort of God do you worship? Behind the scenes, our God is preparing a banquet for you in the presence of your enemies.

Do not panic when your prayers are not answered, do not panic when God does not move when you want Him to. He is working for you. All things work together for good to them that love the Lord. "And, behold, there arose a great tempest in the sea, insomuch that the ship was covered with the waves: but he was asleep, And his disciples came to him, and awoke him, saying, Lord, save us: we perish. And he saith unto them, Why are ye fearful, O ye of little faith? Then he arose and rebuked the winds and the sea, and there was a great calm." **(Matthew 8:24-26 KJV)**

The Bible says one of them said, "who is this man that even the wind obeys him?" Who is this man that

E. S. Isaiah, Ph.D.

even cancer obeys him? Who is this man that poverty, headaches, and other infirmities listen to? What kind of man is this? Maybe you have prayed and given it to God, but the Lord sent me to tell you it is under control. He will surprise people on your behalf and let them know He has the final say and no man can change your destiny. I do not know what kept you all night worrying and crying.

God says before your days on earth are over, He will do something extraordinary in your life. Eyes have not been seen, and neither ears have heard what He is about to do in your life.

Every dry bone in your life will spring forth in the name of Jesus; every barren womb in your life will give birth in the name of Jesus, and every dry hand will begin to spring forth financially in the name of Jesus.

So, why do you not agree today with me in prayer that God can handle whatever situation you are going through? He knows what you are facing and will help you. Trust God!

He asked the blind man, "What should I do for you?" and the blind man answered, "I want to see you again." The Bible says He made spit on the ground and used it to clean the man's eyes, and He said, "go and wash in the pool of Samaria." The blind man knew it was Jesus who was speaking. He knew the Lord of Lords was talking and had to do what He asked him to do.

Many preachers say, "leave your issue at the foot of the cross." This is where issues are solved and problems put to rest. God will take care of them, and you will never

91

have to worry about them anymore. I want to declare and decree a prayer on somebody on the verge of giving up and calling it a day. God says, "I have it under control" Stay strong and do not give up. All will be well. Selah!

PROPHETIC DECLARATIONS

- May the Lord minister to you in your dreams and solve every issue in your life.

- I decree that the glory of God will be seen in your life even amid your struggle and pain.

- I speak peace into your life in all you do.

- You are moving into a greater height and office.

- The favor of God will locate me in all I do.

- I will always be the head and not the tail.

- Failure is not my portion.

CHAPTER FIFTEEN
GOD OF IMPOSSIBILITIES

Many of us have trusted something, maybe the system, politicians, parents, doctors, nurses, lawyers, uncles, and aunties disappoint, but there is a man that can never fail you. There is one man that I have known from birth that can never die. People will disappoint you, and you will put your hands on your head and wish you did not put your trust in them.

But I have come to tell one person that if you trust in Jesus, you will never see any failure; your life will be alright. If you trust in Jesus, He will change things and bring everything dead to life. He will cause a barren woman to live in a house as a mother, and He will bring back restoration in your marriage and make all impossibilities possible.

God is the only one that can change things around. Are they saying that you will no longer live? Are you down to nothing? God is up to something. When your doctor and lawyer say no, our God says yes. God specializes in impossibilities. Our ministers need to have this kind of faith. You have to believe everything will turn out okay even though all hope is lost.

Our God can change what the doctor cannot change. He can transform things in your life that the doctor cannot alter. Our God can change your story and bring you to the front. He can do exceedingly abundantly what we can ask or think. When you place your hands on your head, do people ever complain? I am here to let someone know that our God is an expert at overcoming obstacles. Our God is capable of doing what humans cannot do. I remember a lady who gave a testimony in church. Many people speculated that she would never birth a child, but I told her that our God specializes in impossibilities. On her 37th birthday, God said, "It is now time to shut the mouth of the naysayers." In this world, people will say what they do not know out of imagination. They do not comprehend God's plan and purpose for your life, which is why this is the case.

They will talk and gossip about you. So many people will write you off even before God says it is over. You have people that say this is not going to happen. It is just impossible. Because you cannot excel in school, many people think you are the problem. Listen, **Luke 1:34-37** tells the story of Mary and Elizabeth when the angel of the Lord visited them. So many people thought otherwise, but our God is the God of impossibilities.

For with God, nothing is impossible. Therefore, your case is not hard for God.

Your issues are not hard for God because we have a God who specializes in doing miracles.

I have a God who can move mountains, and I have a God who can heal the sick, I have a God who can raise the dead, I have a God who can make me pass my examination, I have a God who can change my marriage, I have a God who can change my children, I have a God who can change my story.

My God specializes in impossibilities. Thus, I came to tell you that if you doubt God today, I do not want you to question him anymore, for the Bible says, "Write the vision, make it planned that whosoever will read it will run, for the vision is yet for an appointed time."

Your appointed moment has come, and your appointed season is here. Whatever you were unable to accomplish, your time for success has come.

I decree it in the name of Jesus: everything that was impossible in your life will become possible in Jesus' name.

Without God, you will struggle and be unable to do anything positive. I can tell you that life is not about what you see. It is not about what you are going through right now. It is not about what you are facing. Just remember that with God, all things are possible. Do not forget that if you are publicly assertive, you must be secretly prayerful.

The problem in Christendom is that too many Christians are trying to bring down other Christians. We do not care about our brothers and sisters in Christ; as long as the purpose is not one, there is no togetherness.

If you want good things to come your way and to excel in life, you must be willing to help others achieve their goals. If He has not finished with you yet, the amount of tests you are undergoing is not a solution because He is not a God of confusion but purpose. Before He releases you for the next mission, you must complete the goal for which He called you. We encounter difficulties in our walk with God because of this. People's perceptions about you in the church and among your friends should not bother you, but you have to push on and trust in God and not a man because the latter can make you lose and miss your blessing if you cannot focus on God. No matter the pains and hardships you go through, trust Him.

Your focus should be on Jesus, the author, and finisher of our faith, for He is saying, "I am the God of impossibility."

People may hurt you, but I implore you to fix your eyes on Jesus. People may have said many things about you but hear me today. Until you have been talked about, you may not know the value of your anointing. For example, I believe when the angel of the Lord appeared to Mary and told her that she would conceive. Many people talked about her as a prostitute, but that did not bother Mary because she looked up to Jesus.

Have you ever had the experience of hearing others gossip about you and knock you down, and you get to listen to them? But you rejoice in all this because you know you have a God who specializes in the impossible. People may call you a homeless, barren, broken person, or bastard child, but in all this, the Lord says, *"For I know the plans I have for you, that of good and not of evil that I may give you an expected end."* He said I got something I can write about you that will be read in the newspaper for good, bringing you from nothing to something.

Maybe you are crying as you read this message, passing through what you never expected in this life, and people have doubted your ability to excel. Are you about to give up your self-esteem because of people's talk? Today, I came to tell you that our God is a God of impossibilities. Just look up to Him, and He will turn your life around.

I do not know what is disturbing you. I have no idea what you are contemplating at this moment. However, I want to assure you; your story will never remain the same, and your testimony will locate you soon.

Weeping may endure for the night, but joy comes in the morning. Everything God has for you, I decree upon your life. It is delivered to you in the name of Jesus because all things are possible with Him. We must be able to look the enemy in the face and tell him that no matter what we have done, there is still God who can change impossibilities into possibilities. Let it be known that you have a God who specializes in doing the impossible. Trust Him!

CHAPTER SIXTEEN
BELIEVING IT

Extraordinarily, some of us have lost hope that things will not go as planned. Yet, the Scripture in *Romans 8:28 says, "For all things work together for good for them that love the Lord."*

Unwavering faith is a faith that does not shift grounds. Your faith is tested when there are trials, temptations, and tribulations.

The Bible says, "I will lift up mine eyes unto the hills, from whence cometh my help. My help cometh from the LORD, which made heaven and earth. He will not suffer thy foot to be moved: he that keepeth thee will not slumber." (Psalms 121:1 KJV)

I want you to know that this is very profound, and our generation needs unshakeable faith of this kind.

We are in a season where our faith is being tested, our faith is being tried, and our faith must produce a result.

You cannot serve God and not be tested. You cannot serve God and not go through trials and tribulations. "There hath no temptation taken you but such as is common to man: but God is faithful, who will not suffer you to be tempted above that ye are able; but will with the temptation also make a way to escape, that ye may be able to bear it." (I Corinthians 10:13 KJV)

For it is expected, you will have to go through it. If you do not want to go through it, I will ask questions like, what about Job, David, Mordechai, and Esther? All these people had to go through a trial season.

It is easy to believe that God no longer cares about us when we go through a difficult time. As a result, we have come to believe that God is no longer God. But the Bible says, *"He is God even unto the ends of the earth."*

Something profound happened in this Scripture that I want you to note:

As a Christian, you attend church service, go for choir rehearsal, register your presence in the women's meetings, and ask God to do something in your life, and He answers you.

Think about it. It is like back in the days when we used to ask our parents for school fees, and they would answer us with just one word, sometimes acting as if they were not listening.

I do not know if you have the kind of father I have. He appears not to pay attention when you talk to him about money. However, occasionally, he will play the sleeping card to catch you off guard if you say anything out of the ordinary. After that, he suddenly becomes alert and asks you a series of questions.

As humans, you must understand that you will go through seasons and times, and it will feel like Jesus is not there. So, likewise, you will sometimes go through tribulations and hard water in your life, and it will feel as though your prayers are not heard.

I will tell you a story about two girls whose father was wealthy. They lived in Ohio in the early 2000s, and someone paid a kidnapper to kill his two daughters. One of those girls had an early dismissal from school. While she was walking home, unknown to her, the kidnapper was lying in wait for her and had a perfect opportunity to get her, but instead of getting the girl, he ran away and waited for the sister to come. When the sister came, he got hold of her, assaulted and then killed her. The city was in fear, and the police jumped into action to help find the murderer.

When he was finally caught, he was asked, "You were supposed to kill both girls; why did you kill one and allow the other to walk free?" He said, "because when I saw the first one walking down the pathway, there was a man in front of her with a mighty sword in his hand, and I could not just face that man because he looked like Jesus, and I know that this face was not just an ordinary face."

The Bible in *1 John 4:4 says, "Greater is he that is in me, than he that is in the world."*

There is nothing as sweet as working with God. Even amid your storm, he will show up. There will be unwavering faith when dealing with God's things. There is going to be a faith that is untouchable and unshakable. Your faith will be tried and tested, and your faith must stand the test of time. Sometimes in your life, you do not want to take no for an answer. You will tell God, "you said you would bless me, but I want you to know that I need a blessing right now. I refuse to wait another year. I refuse to go back the same way I came. I refuse to go through the struggle. I need you to bless me right here, right now." Genesis. 32:26 says: "I will not let you go until you bless me."

As I thought to myself, besides Samson, whom we all know of, Jacob should have been the strongest man in the Bible. How is it possible for a human to wrestle an angel till the hip socket is broken? He must have been a powerful man, then.

He wrestled with the angel until it was the dawn of day. And the angel said, "Please, let me go." Even the Angel was out of breath, or maybe he was tired. But Jacob said, "I will not let you go," and the angel changed his name.

My question now is, what do you want Jesus to do for you? Giving up is not an option.

You have to press toward the mark. You are not to give up because God has made a promise in your life, "I will bless you, I will lift you, and I will heal you." Hold Him by his word when things are not going right, and He will answer you.

Years ago, a man confided in me, "Man of God, I quit going to church." "Why did you stop?" I questioned him. "None of the things God promised me has come to pass. He does not keep his promises," he retorted.

According to him, nothing in life made sense. I looked at him and asked, "Which is more important right now? Is it to breathe in or out?" His eyes lightened up, and he could not understand where I was going with the question. Immediately, he smiled and said, "Pastor, that is a tough question to answer." Then I reminded him that he could not choose with God. He is all or nothing!

With the breath you have, and in the work you do with your life, you need Jesus. You still need Jesus when things are difficult, good, awful or when things go differently than anticipated.

It is necessary to create unwavering faith. My beloved, the world has changed significantly since the 19th century. Everything has changed.

I assure you that no one nowadays would think we would attend church with our faces covered. And do you know what is funny? The Devil is still pursuing the church despite all these things.

Do you possess the faith that will endure the test of time? Do you own the fortitude to persevere when circumstances aren't ideal? Do you have the willpower to persevere?

Do you possess the fortitude necessary to weather the storm? "I will be with you during the storm," says the Lord. "Thy word is a lamp unto my feet and a light unto my path." Psalm 119:105 KJV)

When you have unwavering faith, it will be put to the test. According to the Bible, one night at Job's house, his servants said, *"Your sons were there having fun in their elder brother's house. The house collapsed, and they all died, and I alone escaped to tell you." And while he was talking, and another came, and another one came, and another one came. But the Bible says Job ripped apart his clothes and said, "Naked I came out of my mother's womb and naked shall I return, the Lord gave and the Lord taketh away, blessed be the name of the Lord." (Job 1:21 KJV)*

How many of us today can claim that? The Lord gives and takes away. If you probably had an accident, lost money, or became unwell, those things will not go away. Someone may claim, "Oh, I do not have to go to church anymore," and they may be mistaken.

The Bible states that Job never denied God. His skin was covered with rashes, yet he clung to God. Thank God Job came out strong and much better than in the beginning. He endured the test of time after being tried and tested. Unfortunately, Christians frequently misunderstand the importance of waiting for God's timing.

We frequently fail to recognize that God's actions toward us are always for our benefit. Jeremiah 29:11

should be often read. He also said, "I knew you and had a plan for you before I made you in the womb." I have specific plans for you.

Hear this! The things you are going through now are not new to God. God knows that you will have to go through this.

A lady came to my church office and said, "Pastor, I have received immigration papers. They told me to come, but I do not think I will go because this is suspicious." So, I asked, "You have been asking to get a green card. What changed?" She replied, "Well, yes, but I will not go." Her reason for the change of mind was still not apparent, and I was moved to ask her another question, "Do you believe in God?" She answered in affirmative, and I told her, "Go, and you will see the hands of God."

Two days later, I was taking some rest at home when my phone rang. It was the lady I had spoken to. As I picked up the call, she said, "Pastor, I have been granted a green card." I asked her, "Did they lock you up?" She said no, and I asked, "Why then were you scared?"

God knows that you will go through this process. He knows that things like this will come and cause you to be afraid.

He said in *Psalm 23:4, "...though I walk through the valley of the shadow of death, I will fear no evil."* For the Lord will go before you, he will be there with you in the midst of the storm. He will prove himself as Lord and king. So why do you have to fear? Where is your faith? The God you serve is the same yesterday, today, and forever.

He will never change. Man will change, friends and neighbors will change, and your parents will change, but God will not.

The Bible says in Matt.17.20: *"And Jesus said unto them, Because of your unbelief: for verily I say unto you, if ye have faith as a grain of mustard seed, ye shall say unto this mountain, Remove hence to yonder place, and it shall remove, and nothing shall be impossible unto you."*

If your faith is small, God will work with what you have.

Twenty years ago, if you had told me I would become a preacher, I would have said no. However, God had other plans for my life that I was unaware of.

When the blessings come, you will forget about the things you had to endure, and you will have to look at something good and genuinely say, I had to rely and stay on God, who has given me the desires of my heart. This will surely be your testimony in the name of Jesus. The Lord shall speak amid your storm. Grace is released for you to go through it, and you will come back with testimonies in Jesus' name.

CHAPTER SEVENTEEN

THE POWER OF I AM

In times of adversaries, not everyone will think of this Scripture, "I can do all things through Christ who strengthens me."

Though we keep speaking about it, many do not mean it. But today, please look at it from another perspective. "I CAN DO ALL THINGS THROUGH CHRIST WHO STRENGTHENETH ME." (Philippians 4:13 KJV)

I am so glad that the Bible did not say, I can do some things, few things, but all things, through Christ.

It is not out of place to call your pastor to pray for you or visit a doctor if you are ill. However, there are situations when you can lay your hands on yourself and declare yourself healed. Your words have power; always keep in mind that YOU CAN!

The Bible says, "I will honor the words that come from your mouth." If you lay your hands on yourself and say, "I am healed," and believe it, God will heal you.

In the story of Moses, God had chosen him to lead the children of Israel out of Egypt. As someone whose faith in God was not strong, Moses doubted the capabilities of God. Nevertheless, God, in his position as the creator of the universe, promised to go with him. The first sign was when God sent him to Pharoah. When Moses appeared before Pharoah, Pharaoh asked, "How do I know that it is God that has sent you?" Moses dropped the rod in the presence of Pharaoh, turning it into a serpent. Pharoah called his magicians, sorcerers, and wise men who did the same thing using their magic powers.

For God to prove that his presence was with Moses, the Bible says his serpent swallowed up all of the magician's serpents, and Moses reached down and grabbed the snake, which became a rod again. God sometimes operates in ways we do not comprehend. We fail to see that we have the ability to perform all of these things. You have the power!

Luke 10:19 (KJV) "Behold, I give unto you power to tread on serpents and scorpions, and over all the power of the enemy: and nothing shall by any means hurt you."

This is the power of I Can. I can overcome every obstacle, every block in front of me, and anything that might stand in my path. I can; you can, we can.

My favorite verse in the Bible, *Exodus 14:13, says, "And Moses said unto the people, Fear ye not, stand still, and see the salvation of the LORD, which he will shew to you today: for the Egyptians whom ye have seen today, ye shall see them again no more forever."*

There is power within, and I want you to know that. The Bible says in **Phil. 2:10:** "That at the name of Jesus, every knee should bow, of things in heaven, and things in earth, and under the ground."

Many people are living in fear due to the world we live in. But the Bible gives us assurances of God's safety at all times.

When I walk into the midst of challenges and situations, I am not just walking because my name is Pastor Isaiah, but because the Lord is with me.

Why would the Bible give us the authority to say, I can do everything? This is because I have the power within me. The three Hebrew boys in *Daniel 3:16 said to the King, "We are not careful to answer you in this matter, but if our God is not able to deliver us from this fire, so be it."*

These guys spoke with the power within them. The King commanded that the furnace be heated ten times more. When you serve God, there will be significant challenges in your life. If you think you will serve God like driving through McDonald's, you are fooling yourself. God is not a drive-through.

When I was reading the Scriptures, I found out that Prophet Isaiah was killed upside down and cut in halves by the orders of Manasseh. Some disciples of Jesus were beheaded, and some were thrown into a pot of oil.

None of the disciples but John died a natural death. During their time on earth, these disciples saw, touched, dined, and communed with Jesus. Why, then, did they die a painful death? Walking with Jesus is not easy.

Serving God will have to take every single breath from you. Some time ago, I spoke to some people and told them you could be widespread and not be known. Make noise all you want and even give your last, but nobody knows you.

When you enter a place, no one immediately acknowledges you. Even when Barack Obama served as the country's first black president, some individuals had no idea who he was. Even today, some people are unaware of Donald Trump's past as president. You will be shocked to learn how much the average person does not know about others. But, due to the presence of God's power within you, you will not need to raise a fuss about some issues in life.

When the power of "I CAN" is within you, it brings revelation. It will reveal the Christ in you. Even when you sit or eat at the same table with people whose hearts are not right with you, the power within will reveal them to you. It will tell you to watch and keep your eyes open. The power of God within you will be able to show things to you.

I can do all things through Christ, which strengthens me. If you do it without Christ, you do it in vain.

Let me tell you what happened to me in Nigeria. One of my friends, a pastor, invited me to come and

110

address some youths in the church. I had no idea I would address the youth who knew their Bible. The session lasted for about an hour, and when I was about to leave, they said, "Not yet, Pastor. We are going to pray for you." The Spirit of God was present in these young people when they began praying. This was the best prayer I have ever received in a year. You will be amazed at how God uses the little things. He uses the youngest person you can't even imagine God could use.

I once saw a video of a seven or six-year-old boy commanding the virus to go away, and people were crying and speaking in tongues. I said, *"God is not moving in a big crowd anymore."* You might be looking for a church filled with many scholars and fancy cars in the parking lot, but frankly, the crowd does not count. Do not get me wrong; I am not saying it is wrong; I am just saying that you should look for a place where the I AM dwells and the hosts of heaven are always there. The power within you must be able to sterilize and pull you out in and out of season.

You must be energetic. You must be active and relevant because the strength within you will not let you down. The power within you will keep you going when everyone else is tired and weary. The strength inside you will restore the knowledge of who Christ is.

The power of "I CAN" will strengthen you. Everybody is sick, but you are still walking boldly. Ask David in the Bible, and he will tell you that you need the power of I AM to win all battles. Nobody knows the key to your strength. Everyone else faces difficulties and obstacles, yet you continue to stand tall. You are strengthened from within. That strength within you speaks for you. Greater is He that is in you than in the world.

The power within you will give you the grace to be strengthened. When others are going down and weary, God is picking you up. When others are tired, God gives you a new feeling and a guide. When others are getting low on gas, God is pumping your gas because there is a power within you that gives you the grace to do everything.

Look at it this way: some people started school with you, and when you walked over the stage at graduation, not all of them did so with you. It may not just be school but anything else. Some people registered in the same class as you, but about two or three had dropped out or withdrew as time passed. Think about it.

The Bible says that race is not given to the strong. Do you know why I love wrestling? I love wrestling because sometimes, it is not the man with the big body and muscles that may end up winning, but a petite man who is his counterpart. The story of David and Goliath gives a perfect illustration.

It's not all about being muscular; it is about the skill. Despite his tiny stature, David overcame Goliath with a stone and a sling. That is the power of I CAN. This power will challenge you, it will reveal, it will strengthen, and it will bring back the glory. If you have been dwelling in the presence of God and you have never felt the presence of God, something is wrong. You need the company of the I AM.

A friend of mine shared a personal story with me. He told me of his father, who was in the bathroom about to take a bath. The man, unfortunately, slipped and fell. When he recovered, he could not walk too well. I asked him what caused the fall, and he replied, "A ghost slapped him." A ghost he could not see, but he felt it.

Another friend here in Texas woke up one morning and discovered that he had something written on his stomach with red ink. He came to church, called me out, and we went inside the Pastor's office. He opened his shirt and said, "Look at this mark." I asked where it came from. And he said he woke up to see it. I wondered what he would do about it. He said they were going to kill him. I could see the fear in his eyes. I told him not to worry because the power of life and death is in the hands of God. I tried to make him understand that no one could kill him. After our discussions, I held his hands and prayed for him. I then told him to get a tissue and clean the mark off. People always want you to take the place of their death and pain.

He went home, and later that night, at about 2 a.m., his wife called to inform me that her husband could not sleep because of what had occurred the previous night. He still believed some unknown forces would murder him in his sleep if they found out he had cleaned the mark.

God has given you power. It is not the power to make noise or the power to fear. It is the power to command that every knee must bow at the mention of the name of Jesus. It did not say some knees, but EVERY KNEE.

Let me share this breathtaking testimony about the power of the I AM. Back home in Nigeria, I remember it as if it were yesterday. I was about seventeen or thereabout. A church member who had just had a baby had scheduled a day for the dedication of the child, and when that day came, everyone was busy cooking and preparing for the crowd that would show up in the morning. But, unbeknownst to everyone else, the child had died that morning.

Everybody was waiting in anticipation. Nobody knew the child was dead.

The mother and father agreed amongst themselves not to create a scene. They kept their cool and still took the dead child to church. When the pastor called upon them to bring the child out for dedication, they danced out excitedly. As she stood before the pastor, tears rushed out of her eyes. The pastor thought it was tears of joy not knowing the child he was about to dedicate was a dead child.

The mother handed the child to the father, and the father passed him to the pastor. The pastor dedicated the child, gave it back to the mother, and returned to officiate the rest of the service.

As he was about to proceed to the next item on the program, the Spirit of God ministered to the pastor and told him of the dead child he had just dedicated. After receiving the revelation, the pastor went to where the child's mother was and placed his thumb on the infant's forehead before returning to the pulpit. Almost immediately, the child sneezed. He came back alive through the power of the I AM.

What no man can do, God can do it. There is power within you. Something inside of you must be able to revive your weakness to tell you that although the situation looks dire, something good is coming. A transformation must occur inside your mind that tells you it does not matter what the doctor said, what the lawyer said, and what your landlord said. Just know that God has the final say.

The Bible records, *"And he awoke out of his sleep, and said, I will go out as at other times before, and shake myself. And he wist not that the LORD had departed from him". (Judges 16:20 KJV)*

Samson had so depended on himself till he disclosed his secret to Delilah. The Devil will come after your peace when you have something important or carry something meaningful in life. The Devil does not just attack an empty vessel. The Devil will only target someone who wears the star of God, someone who has something to offer. So, get on your knees and thank God if you are going through such a phase. The Devil has nothing to do with you if you are empty.

The power of "I CAN" will bring calmness amid your storm if you bear God's anointing. When things do not seem right, the power of "I CAN" will provide tranquility. Just take a seat and declare, "I can do everything through Christ who strengthens me." Change how you think about what I CAN today. Not just a cliché, either. You must have the inner conviction that you can accomplish everything through Christ. You are capable of anything.

When you speak, do not just begin to talk, but speak with confirmation. Speak with boldness, and let the Devil hear you. There is power in your tongue. But, unfortunately, very few of us understand this, and we will always live in fear until we know the power that comes with the word-I AM.

Dear reader, one of the issues we have in Christendom is that many of us become victims due to the things we say and do in our daily lives. We are haunted by the things we have said in the past. However, your words have power, and you will not attract great things until you start being positive. Just know that there is power in your mouth, and when you speak it, God will honor it. Remember, out of the abundance of the heart, the mouth speaketh. We always use this adage, and I have often heard it: "As you make your bed, so you lie on it."

What we say has influence. God has endowed us with the ability and grace to speak, and heaven will honor our words.

May the power of "I CAN" be established in you, knowing that all things are possible with God, and may the Lord help us in Jesus' name.

GOD LOVES STRUCTURE

N ow that you have read the content of this book, I plead with you not to go into ministry without structure. God is a God of structure. Do not expect him to move mountains when you have not yet tested the valley. Stop expecting God to fill up your church pews when you have not done any evangelism. Put a structure in place and make sure it is not what you copied off the internet. Let it be that you have cried out to God in prayers and sought his face for a divine direction. Then and only then will you see His glory and presence. Be reminded that what works for others may NOT work for you and vice versa. Make sure you are not carried away by emotions. Take out time for yourself in prayer and consult your spiritual mentors. Be led by the spirit and not the feeling or the people.

SOLILOQUY 2

THE CONSISTENCY GOSPEL

W hat I have come to see in my experience in ministry and in the course of gathering content, searching materials, books, and interviews in preparation for this book is very shocking, and I must share it with you. But first, our God is a God of consistency. What He said He would do, is what He will do no matter what.

Pastors, Bishops, Prophets, Ministers of the gospel, etc., start so good, but along the line, they fall short. The question is, why? They lost focus on what God called them to do, some became advocates for politicians, and some turned their altars into political grounds and other traditional things.

Please, do not get me wrong. I am all for anyone who welcomes fellow politicians. After all, they are human beings at the end of the day. What I am saying here is that there should be a limit. I have seen pastors who want to become presidents of a nation, activists, etc. How will they run the church of God and the country simultaneously? When God gives a vision to someone, it is tough for another person to execute it.

BE CONSISTENT IN WHATEVER YOU ARE DOING! Lead if God has called you, and use your office wisely. Do not take sides, but give wise counsel. Many political leaders have been misled because of what Men and Women of God had prophesied to them. Some of those things never came to pass, and some of these things were said to get favors from the political figure. Live a holy life, by all means. Let the neighborhood you serve revere you for your principles and the message you teach.

Be who God has called you to be, and be proud to be one. Many preachers started as pastors and later, along the way, became gospel singers, and many gospel ministers are now becoming pastors. Just because God gave you a moment does not mean you now have a ministry to open a church or sing. Preaching is NOT a career. It is a CALLING. If God calls you, we will see when you are consistent in and out of season. Stay faithful to your calling, and make sure no one lures you into something not of God. I am confident and convinced you would be great.

SOLILOQUY 3

LEARN TO ADJUST

The level of spirituality most preachers display shocks me most times. It is so bad that they will not answer you if you greet them because they are always "spiritual." So many of us live headless lives because we cannot separate what we feel from what we know. So many preachers, church workers, Elders, Bishops, Prophets, etc., struggle big time whenever they are taken out of their comfort zone. I have seen many preachers who fumble on the pulpit coming from Africa to minister in Europe or North America. What works in churches in America may not work in Africa, and vice versa.

You have to learn how to adapt and adjust if you want to be a successful preacher. Understand that I am not saying you should change your understanding of God or the word. I am conveying here to let your audience know that you are entirely on board with what they know to be accurate and actual preaching. Anytime I am suitable to sit under my Dad's preaching, I am relaxed and less worried because I know he will deliver as usual regardless of the audience you place him. Many preachers would fail if they removed them from their regular church audience. How flexible are you?

Can you be trusted to execute an assignment without fumbling? A young, vibrant preacher was invited to say a closing prayer at a state banquet at the government house. Knowing fully well that he was one of the best preachers in the city as of those days, the august crowd was expectant. Some refused to leave because they wanted to hear him pray. When that moment finally came, the tuxedo-suited preacher walked up to the podium with his bodyguards surrounding him as if he was a target to be assassinated. When he stepped to the microphone, the young preacher lost it all. He started telling stories and spent almost twenty minutes acknowledging the guest and the dignitaries. Finally, they were tired from sitting, and the lengthy program lapsed into the early morning hours.

The closing prayer, slated to take less than ten minutes, went all the way to thirty-two minutes. The special guest and some dignitaries walked out to crown it all while the Pentecostal preacher was busy appreciating the crowd. He had become a disappointment to many. Some thought he must have been under the weather, while others thought he was carried away. I know you would love to hear my conclusion about what happened to the preacher. I sincerely believe he was taken out of his comfort zone and lost everything because he had never operated in such an atmosphere.

I am way above my thirties now and have not heard of or seen that man being invited to any government function after that embarrassing moment. One of the things I share with our church members all the time is that I am not called only to the Apostolic church, I may have been ordained in the church, but I am a Shepherd of God's sheep, which includes ALL sheep. So to prevent it from being a problem for you, learn to adjust.

I HOPE YOU FAIL

In a world where men and women are competing for relevance, and our altars have been polluted with some strange things, there is one thing I hope and pray for. I hope you fail! Some people may be curious as to why I would compose a page-long soliloquy in the hopes that someone would fail in a book meant to be uplifting and consoling.

Before you get all worked out, relax and breathe! If you leave God or decide to add anything that is not God to your altar, to deceive, or lie to the people of God, this is where my prayer comes to play. I hope you fail. Anyone who wants to see the glory of God in their life must work hard and pray.

Notwithstanding, certain people no longer believe in praying or waiting on God. Instead, they want an easy way out. They love the crowds and the pump, but deep inside their hearts, they are operating with some strange powers. I wish, above all things, that you fail.

EPILOGUE

Somewhere in your reach, you have come across somebody who once used to be in church, sang in the choir, or was a dedicated prayer warrior, and along the line, they failed. What have we done to this generation? Have you noticed that most or maybe one-third of all secular artists were once in church? Without mentioning names, check them, and read their biography. Some of them are preachers' kids to this day. If we only preach to the same groups of persons every Sunday and midweek service, we are doing a disservice to Christianity. Our work is to go into the world and win souls for Christ. Somebody out there needs to know and hear God. I dare you to do it.

This book points to the struggles of every minister in the ministry. It also highlights the errors we make frequently and how to avoid them. Of course, God wants something better for us as ministers of the gospel, but the key to enjoying a better life in the church lies in the hands of the minister.

Therefore, as you close this book and pick up the next one, you will realize that I have encouraged you, poured water on you, and dressed your wounds. I am sending you to the battlefield to finish the fight and finish strong! You may have seen or encountered something in this book that has motivated you to do something different. But permit me to say this to you; God will no longer allow the ministers of this time to mishandle His presence. I pray that God will start embarrassing ministers who keep mishandling His presence. The presence of God is the only thing that has the power to heal, bless, and restore people. I am speaking to the glory carriers and the glory chasers, people who will say, all I want is to see the glory of God. I am tired of fakeness in the church, and I like the presence of God and nothing else.

After reading this book with a deep spiritual understanding, I am confident you must have concluded what God wants and expects from you.

I hope to see you at the top!

www.ingramcontent.com/pod-product-compliance
Lightning Source LLC
Chambersburg PA
CBHW060144100426
42744CB00007B/895